More Than a Conqueror

Ryan Shieh

Table of Contents

Introduction   9

Chapter 1: Step Back   15

Chapter 2: Living With an Open Heart   33

Chapter 3: Greater is He   43

Chapter 4: Faith Talks   55

Chapter 5: Virtues of Love, Virtues of Fear   81

Chapter 6: Finding Your Purpose   99

Chapter 7: Work for the Good   109

Chapter 8: Meaningless   123

Chapter 9: An Act of Love   133

Chapter 10: Final Thoughts   139

Favorite Verses Section   145

Acknowledgements   149

About the Author   151

To my greatest role models,
who have guided and supported me from the beginning.
Thank you, Mom and Dad!

Introduction

What's up! My name is Ryan and I'm so excited you have opened up this book. I pray that these words you read will help and guide you through some of your current situations and emotions.

I wrote this book with a sole purpose of explaining my personal point of view and experiences with my faith in Jesus. I don't want to get too far into it so early on, but my life has truly changed for the better when I put Christ at the forefront. I hope that this book will help change yours too, if you have not already done so.

As a kid I was raised by my Mom and Dad to respect and love others, give your best, and bring positivity. It's not ironic that these are the same principles Jesus has for us when dealing with one another. Besides salvation, which we will get into, our impact on others through Christ is very important.

Let's look at our lives. We all have a choice everyday to get out of bed, drink a cup of coffee, be nice to a stranger, make a decision we shouldn't, the list goes on. There are so many things we are able to do, whether they have positive or negative effects on us and others as well.

One day at school, as I was grabbing my lunch, an announcement was made describing how we would be forced to close for a significant amount of time due to the COVID-19 outbreak. A virus so scary and tragic that we had to shut down, knowing it took the lives of countless individuals.

I went to my usual check out line; my go-to because of the lady who works the register. I won't give her name, but she has such a genuine heart. You always see her with a smile or laugh on her face, and can count on her to ask how you are doing. She always puts others before herself.

Oftentimes I recall seeing her walk to the bus stop right outside of the school. She can't afford her own transportation.

After paying for my meal, I grabbed a 20 dollar bill out of my wallet and slipped it in her hand. I said, "This is for you. I know there is a tough time coming up where you guys won't get paid. Thank you for your countless acts of love towards me and everyone here." As she took the gift, she teared up, gave me a big hug and said thank you.

I'm so glad that I have the opportunity to know this lady and be in a position where I can help her. God really uses her heart to touch others, and she is someone who deserves the world. I'm not saying we have to give money to every person we see in need, but acts of kindness can change someone's day, or even their life. You never know the challenges people are facing in their lives.

We all have a choice everyday to choose love or choose fear. We all have a choice to spread life to others, or drain it. We all have a choice to put others first, instead of putting ourselves first.

There is a reason why we can choose to live selflessly. There is reasoning behind showing love to people who are so trapped in hate. There is someone who put you first before Himself, even when we have countlessly turned against Him.

He is Jesus Christ.

God loves you and I so much that He sent His only Son to die in our place. Jesus already took all of our sins. His death on the cross gives us life- *forever.*

So how can I attain Jesus Christ?

This book was written not only to give people an idea of how to find God but how to live for Him. As you read, try to open your hearts and step out onto the water where God is awaiting you. He has plans for you far beyond your imagination! All it takes is some trust.

When Jesus is at the center of our lives, there is no limit to how much we can achieve. It doesn't take a lot and it doesn't take a miracle. He loves you so much.

He will change your life. Let's get started!

Chapter 1: Step Back

"God's work done in God's way will never lack God's supplies." - **Hudson Taylor**

Growing up, baseball was always a forefront for me and my brother, David. I can't tell you how many hours, days, and weekends were spent on baseball related activities. I participated in both little league and county ball, and joined a travel team once I entered middle school. This was around the time I was figuring out the game and started really enjoying playing it.

During my 8th grade year I had to decide where to attend high school, and I narrowed it down to Riverdale Baptist or Bishop McNamara. Riverdale had a nationally ranked program, but I would have more playtime as a freshman at McNamara.

Ultimately I decided on Riverdale and felt God was pulling me in that direction. The coaches were faith driven and helped me grow my relationship with Christ. They were true leaders and have a special place in my heart.

I knew going into the fall I probably would not see a lot of playtime as catcher on the varsity field. There were two guys ahead of me, both very talented and I was the youngest. I told myself I would show up everyday and compete while trying to learn from my older and more experienced teammates.

In life, we should never stop learning and growing mentally. Proverbs 12:1 says, "Whoever loves discipline loves knowledge, but he who hates correction is stupid." Put your pride aside and learn from those who have been there. Don't catch yourself hiding your heart from knowledge.

In November of my freshman year, I found out one of the catchers seriously hurt his arm. The injury required surgery and would limit his time on the field his senior year.

This naturally opened up a spot for me as the backup varsity catcher. I wanted to be a good teammate and push the guys to be their best. I got better from watching and learning from my teammates.

About 2 weeks later, the now starting catcher got expelled from school. Lo and behold, I was the starting catcher for Riverdale Baptist! This was something I never dreamed of achieving as a freshman. My teammates were counting on me and I wanted to help them in any way I could.

Freshman year was life changing for my faith. I was in a classroom setting where my peers were distracted and straying from God's Word. I was in a situation where I could have abandoned God and said, "this road is easier." But faith is made to be strong. God never promises easy roads but He knows our final destination. We all have expected ends from Him full of prosperity and love (Jeremiah 29:11).

We dominated the season finishing 32-1. We took a trip to Puerto Rico, won a championship in Hartsville, South Carolina (very important trip!), and sat #2 in USA Today's National Rankings. This feat was accomplished through teamwork, never relying on any individual but always trusting one another. And of course, we knew God's plan came before any of our baseball careers.

Before the last week of rankings came out, we had already completed our season. The #1 seed though, a high school in Florida, had one game left to play. It was a conference game against a team they beat earlier in the season. My teammates and I were very proud and grateful for our successful season but we still kept track of their game. We had to!

The next day at school, our coach called us in to tell us that somehow the #1 ranked team lost their game, which made Riverdale Baptist #1 in the nation. What are the chances!

If you told me mid eighth-grade year that I would be a national champion in a year, I would have called you crazy. The decision to attend Riverdale was solely based on the opportunity to grow in my relationship with Christ through the strong convictions of my coaches. And looking back, everything panned out perfectly. We followed God's guidance and glorified Him through our actions.

Throughout our lives, we will find ourselves making decisions in many different scenarios. Some easy, some life changing. The best way to deal with this is to put God's intentions first, set aside our own wants and remind ourselves that God has the ultimate plan. He knows far more than we can ever imagine.

Stepping Out Of Our Comfort Zone

During our trip to Puerto Rico, we played a few ball games but our main objective was to share the Gospel. We brought numerous Spanish translated Bibles for distribution and eagerly anticipated what God had in store. I was excited to spread the Word to those who may never have heard it before.

Earlier in the year, Hurricane Maria wiped out a majority of Puerto Rico. This storm killed over 3000 people, changing the lives of countless individuals.

As we flew over the island, there was an array of blue tarps covering the tops of many houses. Months after the storm, families continued to struggle with shelter and had limited resources. Seeing this quality of life really put into perspective how good we have it.

Along with scheduled games, we visited an orphanage in the city of Bayamón. As we got there a bunch of kids came bursting out with big smiles on their faces. For a child who doesn't have a mom or dad figure in their life, I'm sure seeing all of us touched their hearts. I know it touched mine for sure.

Throughout the trip, we passed out hundreds of Bibles and shared Christ to a community that needed Him most. We used this trip as an opportunity to show God's love and remind the people of Puerto Rico that He had not forgotten them. Through the midst of a storm, God's love and care will never fail.

Something we are called to do is be disciples of Christ. According to Mark, we are supposed to "go into all of the world and preach the gospel to all creation" (16:15). This is a *huge* task! It's not easy spreading the Word of God, especially to complete strangers.

Frequently we ask ourselves, "where do we start?" One of the easiest ways to show God's love is through our actions. The way we treat people and our immediate impact can change someone's day... or even life (explained more in Chapter 4).

The main way to influence people towards God is to promote salvation. One must know God to see God, and that comes through faith. Sharing the story of His death, His resurrection, and His love for everyone will ultimately bring people to Christ.

During the trip in South Carolina, we had some down time in our hotel rooms. My roommates included Jose, the kid with the hurt arm, and a kid from the Dominican Republic named Roberto. We also had a pitcher named Noah, who we called Fid. Our room was full of energy.

One night during our team Bible study, I noticed Roberto didn't understand a word being said because he only spoke Spanish. A couple hours passed as I kept thinking about Roberto. It was getting late and the next day we had a big game, however I was still feeling something in my heart. I kept getting this nudge to talk with Roberto about Jesus. I was curious if there was a relationship.

My first thought was to say something, but then remembered he couldn't understand me. I then pulled out my phone and typed into a spanish translator. We now had the ability to communicate! I asked Roberto about Jesus and if he knew how much He loved him. I told him that Jesus died on the cross for our sins so we can have a chance to live forever. Roberto was very attentive and seemed eager to learn more!

He typed into the translator asking how he could have a relationship with God. I explained that through His grace, God wants a relationship with us. Once we repent and ask for forgiveness of our sins, Jesus will come into our hearts.

He wanted to pray! Through the translator we said a simple prayer, asking God to come into Roberto's heart and work in his life. I said, "He loves you Roberto."

He went to the corner of the room, got down on his knees and humbled himself before God. Fid turned to me and said, "What is he doing?" I responded with, "He is repenting to God, right now! This is crazy, man!"

After Roberto gave his life to Christ that night, he wanted to get baptized in front of a community. The Sunday we got back, he was baptized at Riverdale's church with the whole team there to support him. I get teary eyed just thinking about it.

I talked to Fid a few days before writing this chapter. He remembered everything so vividly and it brought back so many memories. Who would have thought that night in a South Carolina hotel room, Roberto would give his life to Jesus?

Fid and I also talked about his own walk with Christ. He recalled a lot of things he had done in his life that he regretted, and remembered at one point thinking God would never forgive him. He thought he was too far gone. But when he accepted Christ himself, he was reminded that God heals the weak and loves the humble. God wants us to come to Him as we are, broken and in need of healing. He mends our broken hearts to make us new!

When God is tugging on your sleeve in a certain situation, make sure to stay in that moment! We never want to miss what He is showing us because even the smallest of things can change one's life. Instead of chasing what our hearts are searching for, remind yourself the true reason for our existence. The true meaning of life is the impact we have on others.

New Beginnings

Throughout the year, there was strife between the school administration and the baseball team. Once the season concluded, the coaches felt like God was leading them elsewhere. The head coach stepped down which left us with no coach for the next year. That year marked the end of an era. Aside from the graduating seniors, the rest of the team ended up transferring to various other schools.

Being a freshman, I had three more years of high school! It was the toughest on me because most of the team were seniors so this was their last year anyway.

Ever since middle school, I always had a good relationship with the McNamara head coach. His name was Coach Sos.

I liked Coach Sos. A lot. Throughout the whole recruiting process for high school, he was not only a coach to me but a mentor. I trusted him so I reached out to him.

Long story short, I was to continue high school at Bishop McNamara. Coach Sos kept a spot in his heart open for me and welcomed me in. I'm so thankful for how it all turned out.

Let's look back at my eighth grade decision: which high school would I attend? In the midst of that process, I weighed the pros and cons of each school, never thinking I would eventually go to *both*. God knew exactly what He was doing. I would grow in my faith at Riverdale and then transfer to McNamara ready to serve the community. His plan. Greater than we think.

As soon as I made the decision to transfer, Coach Sos immediately got on the phone with colleges. He didn't have to do this but he did, even after I bailed on him the previous year.

Fast forward to the fall of 2018. After a fairly successful freshman year, I committed to the University of Maryland. With Maryland close to home, I was impressed with the school and humbled by receiving an offer. I was extremely grateful to be able to commit to a college at such an early point, but recognized that there was still plenty of work to be done.

For the next few months, I started to question my decision to attend Maryland. I didn't fit in with the other commits and didn't feel much of a connection with some of the coaches. It just didn't feel right. I prayed. A lot. God, talk to me. Is this where I need to be? Is this somewhere you can use my life to its fullest? *Show me.*

I started thinking about some alternatives. Do I decommit? Am I jumping to conclusions? I'm not sure how this will be taken by my family. What do I do?

About a year later, I decommitted from Maryland.

I felt in my heart that Maryland was not the best fit for me. At that moment, it seemed as if I made a decision that would negatively affect me in the future. I turned down a good scholarship and was now back searching for another college. Everything seemed like it was falling apart.

Something we all struggle with is worry. We worry about tomorrow, worry about our jobs, our money, our relationships, and our futures. We try to take matters into our own hands and gain control of our lives.

When the God of the universe is on our side, there is nothing more you can do than trust Him! Whatever happens, I know that God will use my situation to the greatest of His glory. I know that through it all, it's not about where I end up. It doesn't matter what college I go to. I know that God will not only lead me, but put me in the perfect spot to impact others through love.

This is what kept me at peace with my decision to decommit. At the time, I could have doubted myself and lost trust in God. I could have panicked and viewed my decision as the wrong one. But I knew that God had me. God loves each and every one of us and will always lead us to His intended path. It's up to us whether or not we take it.

A few months passed and I had been in contact with several colleges. This was around December, so no games were going on. We narrowed it down to a few local colleges. In January, we decided to attend camps at West Virginia University and Liberty University.

Liberty's camp was first. We got there and everything seemed great. Although it was rainy on and off that day, the field was gorgeous. I threw and hit well, and afterwards they gave me a tour of the campus. I then spoke with the head coach, Scott Jackson, and he gave me an offer.

Coach Jackson was very understanding and told me that I didn't need to make a decision immediately. I was to attend the West Virginia camp the following week. I had been in contact with the coaching staff at West Virginia long before Liberty came into the picture, so my natural inclination was to attend West Virginia if everything fell into place at their camp. But after the incredible experience at Liberty, it made the decision a much tougher one.

I remember I was super excited to get out in front of the West Virginia coaching staff. I also remember it was super cold! We got to campus and the facility was insane. After a greeting from the coach, the camp started and basically lasted all day. I showed well and spoke with each coach quite a bit. They told me we would have a conversation later that week.

The next week at school was a little nerve racking. I had a decision to make and wanted to know all of the details right at that moment. I was thinking about it a lot.

On the Wednesday of that week, I was sitting in Spanish class. Just before the bell rang, I received a text from the West Virginia coach. He was ready to talk. I begged my teacher to have a couple minutes so I could call the coach. Thankfully she said "no problem."

The call lasted about 20 minutes. He started off by talking about the kind of player I was and how much he liked me. Cool.

He then told me there literally was no money left for the 2021 class, and I would have to be a recruited walk on. There were no more baseball scholarships available. After the call, much to my disappointment, a lot of thoughts began running through my mind. I thought back to why I decommitted from Maryland and wanted to make my next decision based on the hope of developing closer relationships with my future teammates and coaches. I talked to my family about it and we were all on the same page. Financially speaking, there was the obvious choice, but we also felt a stronger connection with one of the schools. I called Coach Jackson and eagerly committed to Liberty University.

There will be plenty of decisions we make throughout our lives that will dictate our future. To me, choosing a college is not a life-changing decision; nothing compared to moving your family to a foreign country for a job or deciding to continue cancer treatments. But I had to make a decision. At first, I was caught up in the glamour and hype of West Virginia. I thought it would be a better fit than Liberty. But God's plans are far greater than what we can imagine. The lack of scholarship money was God telling me, "Liberty is where you need to be. I need you right here to work for me. I have a plan for you here that is so great you can't even fathom. I hold your life in My hand."

Looking back, I am so thankful for how it worked out. I have great relationships with all of the coaches there, especially Coach Jackson. Not only do we continue to grow in our own relationship, but together we grow our relationship with Christ.

When God throws you a bone- take it. Listen to His guidance. He is the Creator of the universe! He promises that He will lead you on a path of righteousness. There is no plan greater than His. When we need guidance in any aspect of our life, seek God first. Not only will you find yourself in a good situation, but you'll see more opportunities to further His kingdom.

Breaking Out!

After my commitment at the end of January, my team and I had about a month and a half to prepare for the season. We had put in hard work since October and were eager to get onto the field and play. As March 8 rolled around, we prepped for our first game the following day.

It was as beautiful as it could have been in March. We all were excited and came out firing, starting off the season with a win. We were scheduled to leave for a weekend trip the next Friday.

Except that trip would not happen. A couple days before what would have been our departure, all schools and activities were shut down because of the Coronavirus. Our trip was cancelled and school would be out for at least 2 weeks. Great.

There were mixed emotions at that time for a lot of people. Some were scared, some were happy to get free off days from school, some had no opinion. But something we all felt was worry. We worried about the season, worried about this new virus that was being introduced, and worried about the unknown future. It was a scary first couple of days.

Because the virus was so new and held so much uncertainty, there was no time stamp on when we would return to school. From now on we would basically have all day each day to ourselves. With that came a lot of free time, inspiring me to write this book. While the season ended up not happening, I was glad I had an opportunity to complete this book. The break from school may have seemed like a storm, but reality is that was just a way for society to calm down and take a step back. Breathe. Relax. Everything is going to work out.

One of my favorite verses fit perfectly in that time of stress. It comes from Philippians 4:4-7 which reads:

"Rejoice in the Lord always. Again I will say, Rejoice!
Let your gentleness be known to all men. The Lord is at hand.
Be anxious for nothing but in everything by prayer and
supplication, with thanksgiving, let your requests be made
known to God: and the peace of God, which surpasses all

understanding, will guard your hearts and minds through Christ Jesus."

Anxious for nothing. Read that again. We may ask ourselves, "But God, how can we be anxious about nothing when *something* is always presented?"

The truth is, Jesus is why we are able to rejoice. Jesus is how we can remain calm in the midst of a storm. Because He died on the cross for me and you, we have a shot at eternal life. He defeated death when He rose again. That is the greatest gift we can ask for! If we truly believe this, any obstacle or struggle we may face will not faze us. Understand that your eternity is already won. Although you may face trials in this world, the heaven that lasts forever provides peace.

It's not easy to be anxious for nothing. Failing a test or running late for work is stressful. Losing a loved one or filing for divorce is even harder. But, these things are all of the temporary world. Instead of worrying about the now, choose to remember the glory heaven will bring- *forever.* Eternity is where we really want to be.

Now this understanding will take some stepping out of your comfort zone. It's hard telling yourself to relax when you are running late. It's hard to stay calm in the midst of an economic crisis. And the truth is, we become anxious because we truly care about it. We worry about death because we love people. We worry about the world in a global pandemic because we do care for them.

Being anxious for nothing does not mean to stop caring. We need to put our care and love into everything. But, we can't allow the end result to shake us. No matter what happens, it is important to remind ourselves God is at work. He has created the universe in the most perfect way possible. If that is the case, then everything must work for the good. Everything must relate to that final destination of peace. We as people can't change that; God is far too powerful.

That is why we can be anxious for nothing. No matter the storms we face, there will always be a rainbow at the end. It's also how we are conquerors through Christ. He changes our hearts to think in a way most do not. God truly can give you peace. Cast your cares on Him and lean not on your own understanding. He has a greater plan.

In This Game, We Are the Pieces

Some of us live under the illusion that we have control over the rest of our lives. Because we think this way, we hold on tight to all of our things, limiting them from other people. We hide our hearts, guard our resources, keep our own time, hoard our money, the list can go on. The focus is so on ourselves and our wellbeing, we lose chances to step in for those who really need help.

Reality is, we don't control our lives. What we do now is not going to dictate what kind of car we own in 50 years. The workouts we do now will not guarantee us a career of being a professional athlete. While doing these things may push you in that direction, ultimately they do not control the outcome. God holds this world and everything in it. He is who makes it go round and operate in its purest form, where everything works together perfectly.

Something we must come to realize is that wherever God takes us, He will take us. We will be given spots and opportunities from Him where He thinks we will have the most impact. Our job is not to fight for our own wants, but to excel in what He provides. He promises a plan of guidance and prosperity for our lives. Whether we agree with Him or not, ultimately we know that His way is the most effective. He is a see-all, know-all God. Wherever He puts you, that is where you will be the most beneficial. So in that case, use what you have been given to its fullest. Bring positivity to that 9-5 desk job. Show hope to your fellow coworkers who are living check to check. Don't fight His plan, instead trust it.

As a result of choosing trust, we ultimately will not live as selfish and conceited. We will give more and take less. We will love our enemies. We will choose hope instead of hate.

On this cold afternoon, my friends and I were heading to the gym to play basketball. We just finished our workout and we all were hungry so we went downtown for some grub. After our meal we walked outside and this woman approached one of my friends, asking him for money.

Now I'm sure we all have the same universal thought process about giving money to the homeless- we have no idea where the money is going. They could be using the money to buy drugs. They could be using the money to buy alcohol. Or, they could be using it for actual food because they are hungry. You never really know.

In this instance, my friend had no idea where the money was going to go, so he asked her. "I'm sure you are hungry, would you like me to buy you some food?" Instead of dismissing her altogether because of his lack of knowledge, he invested his time into her request and searched for the truth. She told him yes and was desperately in need for a meal. My friend walked her into the Popeyes that was close to us, and after five minutes she came out with a big box of chicken and a smile on her face.

Just like that, her day was impacted. She was able to eat. If my friend was so caught up in himself, and instead sought to only provide for his own needs, this woman would have never eaten. But he realized that his money means nothing, and she needs it more than he does. He gave up control of his life and in turn, watched how it benefited someone else who truly needed it.

It's so easy to get caught up in life and ignore situations where we might be needed. If we live thinking we control our lives, our decisions will be affected this way, and we will not be as selfless and caring for others. We will only care for ourselves. But if we live knowing God is in control, we will give all we have to Him, and in turn watch how He uses us to benefit those around us. Don't wait for opportunities to come only when you feel like it. Live with an open heart and invest your time in others, and God will step up. He always does.

Chapter 2: Living With an Open Heart

"You are the only Bible some unbelievers will ever read." - **John MacArthur**

Throughout this book you will read a lot of different things. Whether it be loving others, trusting God in the midst of a storm, or even working hard, all of this stuff is written based on past experience. I write to try to assist you in your life, since I have attempted and grown from these things myself.

I accepted Christ at a young age and have always been devoted to my faith. I realized that my life's accomplishments truly do not matter as much as I think they do. I am not more important than someone else, nor do I have more value. My life is truly God's because He is who gives it to me. I fall short and He picks me up, everytime. The least I can do is give Him the glory.

These things you will soon read about are what I have tried to do over the course of my life so far. Putting others first, choosing humility, not getting caught up in material things- these are all things God tells us to do.

These life recommendations all have a greater meaning. We don't live selflessly to expect things in return. We don't humble ourselves so someone else can brag about us. We don't love others just to say we loved them. We live like Jesus because Jesus is why we live.

As Christians, we learn that Jesus put others before Himself out of love. Jesus understood that God, His Father, is love and wants to see all of His creation love each other. We are given life through Jesus because of love, so in turn we are expected to love those around us.

The reason I have given my life to Jesus is truly because of His love. I understand that a loving King came to a sinful earth and lived a sinless life. He bore my sins on the cross because He wants to forever live with me in heaven. I cannot fathom why He would do such a thing; the only answer is because He loves me. Because of that, the least I can do is live a loving life for others.

In the Bible there are many scriptures that relate to our good works. Now our salvation isn't earned through our works, because Jesus gives us grace as a gift. But, we do have a job once we accept Jesus to help bring His grace to others. These are examples of the "why" we choose to put others first:

"In the same way, let your light shine before others, so that they may see your good works and give glory to your Father who is in heaven." Matthew 5:16

"And let us not grow weary of doing good, for in due season we will reap, if we do not give up." Galatians 6:9

"For we are his workmanship, created in Christ Jesus for good works, which God prepared beforehand, that we should walk in them." Ephesians 2:10

"And whoever exalts himself will be humbled, and he who humbles himself will be exalted." Matthew 23:12

"Trust in the Lord with all your heart and lean not on your own understanding; in all your ways acknowledge Him, and He will make your path straight." Proverbs 3:5-6

All of these verses center around a similar aspect about our works. If we live for Christ, in turn He will give us life. When we choose to glorify Him, He will guide our paths to be straight. When we give our lives to God and give Him full control, it is only then when He fully provides what He has been holding in store for us.

Now I'm not saying to be expecting a new TV if you are nice to your sister for a week. As I said before, we don't love just to say we love. We love from the goodness of our hearts, just as Jesus did. If the Son of Man chooses to love you selflessly, we have no excuse not to do the same to others.

You may be in a current situation of comfort. You may have all you ever want in life, but you are putting down the people around you. You are bringing negativity to the table. That is the complete opposite of how it should be! Don't get it twisted. Our impact on others means more than our material goods. I offer these things to you based off of my experience with God guiding me. I see Him work in my life everyday. Watching Him use my life to help other people is so humbling, and goes to show what power you can truly hold when the King of Kings lives in your heart.

So, I challenge you. I challenge you to step out of your comfort zone. Having the courage to put others before you is not easy, but I promise it will benefit both sides when it is all said and done. We love because He first loved us. Our lives hold so much significance. We were made to thrive! Take control of your motives and decisions and empower them with love. I pray these things will help and guide you to choose love and gratitude.

Our Salvation

We have all heard the saying "live in the present." While this saying is great for stress relieving and comforting, it does not grasp onto a bigger picture we all have to think about. The truth is, there is more to just life in the present.

What happens after we die?

As much as we don't want to think about it, at some point we are all going to pass this life. It's inevitable. As Christians, we believe in the Bible. What does the Bible say about life after death?

"Nevertheless we, according to his promise, look for new heavens and a new earth, wherein dwelleth righteousness."
2 Peter 3:13

"And Jesus said unto him, Verily I say unto thee, Today shalt thou be with me in paradise." Luke 23:43

"That if thou shalt confess with thy mouth the Lord Jesus, and shalt believe in thine heart that God hath raised him from the dead, thou shalt be saved." Romans 10:9

God promises life after death in Heaven to those who call on Jesus. Why? Because Jesus came to save man from sin. If you want to dig deeper into this right now, I encourage you to turn to Chapter 9.

The truth is, what really matters is our life in eternity. We have two very distinct options- Heaven or Hell. As a Christian, not only do we seek eternity in Heaven, but we must seek it for others as well. We are all called to be disciples of Christ, and explaining God's grace to others is the beginning of one's relationship with Him.

Because of God's love, we are able to be free from sin. We cannot earn salvation and have no right to it. It is a free gift. Not one sin has taken away from my salvation, nor has any good deed added to it. This is a testimony to His grace and forgiveness for all of man, who has countlessly turned against His perfect ways.

This truth allows gratitude to rule our lives. We are humbled because we know there is no reason to boast. We have fallen short, but He has picked us up. In turn, we give our all and live for Him.

Spreading Love, not Fighting Evil

Spreading faith, hope, and love is something we are called to do, and must act upon. However, fighting evil is something we are supposed to flee, to let God fight these battles for us. There is a major difference between the two that can very easily be misinterpreted.

When things happen that are unfair, unjust, and uncalled for, there are two things we can do. We can fight back and add to the problem itself, or respond with love. Responding with love will promote justice and peace while fighting the evil head on will add anger and hate.

Evil is simply far too powerful for us. We see that in our sin; we fall short every single time. Evil will only grow when we fight it, because our attention and concentration is centered upon it. But if we flee evil, we no longer can be a part of the problem. We flee sin by choosing love over hate.

Yes, we need to stand up for what's right. Yes, we need to defend the poor and vulnerable. Yes, we must long for peace and love. But adding to the fire will only make it grow. Fighting with an ego or hate in your heart for another person will only lead to making irrational, hurtful decisions. We are taught to love our neighbors and turn the other cheek. As hard as it may be, doing so takes the battle out of our hands and gives it to a sovereign, all-powerful God.

Take the story when Satan tried to tempt Jesus. When Satan bashed Him with riddles and harsh words, Jesus simply quoted Scripture. He didn't fight Satan and try to overpower Him. Although He could've, He showed us that the true dismissal of evil comes from love.

Choosing love in these situations is not easy, but will guarantee a better outcome than fighting evil. Leave evil alone. Let evil take over this temporary world, because it will; sin allows it to. In the end God will take care of it once and for all. We can stand strong on that promise and spread love in the meantime to those who desperately need it.

Guilt

It's a Friday night. You've been out partying all night and had a couple of drinks. No big deal. The only problem is you remember you promised your parents you wouldn't get drunk, and now you can't even walk straight. Now a wave of guilt crashes over your heart. You're a failure.

This may not be your story, but we have all made mistakes. You didn't pay for that candy bar in the lunch line. You cheated on a test that you said you weren't going to cheat on. You hooked up with some guy at a party that your boyfriend wasn't at. And now there is a tsunami of guilt heading your way.

As Christians we have to do our best to stay away from these things. Staying loyal and having integrity is a big part of character, and people look at you to see how you will react. You don't want to leave a bad impression on someone who is looking for some positivity.

But reality is, we are going to fail. Over and over again. We are sinners who have turned away from God and journeyed down our own paths. We are wrong.

That is where the beauty of God's grace comes in. There must be a balance in our thought process because, while we have sinned severely, God's grace is far more powerful. What

Jesus did on the cross is undeniable and your sin will not change how much He loves you. Because of Him, we are made clean.

This is not to say that when we sin, we do so without thinking twice. Our faith is not genuine if we choose to fail at the same thing over and over again without any remorse. But, we must realize the power of the cross. If we only focus on our wrongs and how sinful we are, we are choosing selfishness. All we care about is ourselves and how we can make up for it, which usually leads to more temptations and opportunities for failure. We must remember the grace that has been given as a gift. Doing so will not only remind you of God's beauty, but will open your heart up to more people. You cannot positively impact someone else when all you focus on is yourself.

You are not defined by your failures, by other people's opinions, or by your status in society. You're not even defined by your particular career field. But you are defined as one thing. A child of a loving, sovereign God.

We will fall short. Every day. We are sinners. But we are also forgiven. There is much more power in His grace than our sin, and if we choose to focus on that alone, we will live with more gratitude than guilt.

"Therefore if any man be in Christ, he is a new creature: old things are passed away; behold, all things are become new."
2 Corinthians 5:17

Chapter 3:
Greater is He

"God will meet you where you are in order to take you where He wants you to go." **- Tony Evans**

One of my favorite Bible stories comes from Matthew 14, describing Jesus walking on water. Jesus just finished ministering to a crowd, thentn told his disciples to take a boat to the next town where He would meet them after He prayed. As the disciples went out toto sea, a storm began to rage and the waters were getting rough. All of a sudden, a disciple saw something walking on the water and called it a ghost. Little did he know that it was Jesus.

Jesus shouted, "Fear not!" and told Peter to come out on the water. Peter obeyed, but as he began to take his steps he was distracted by the crashing waves around him. The storm had taken his focus off of Jesus, and he began to sink. Jesus grabbed him and asked, "You of little faith, why did you doubt?"

When life throws a storm at us, our usual first reaction is to panic. We choose to find ways we can control the storm in hopes of settling it down. Instead of letting Jesus take care of our battles, we opt to fight them by ourselves.

In Romans, God describes how all will work for the good for those who love Him (Romans 8:28). If God promises an expected end, then whatever happens in the middle of that journey will always work for the good! There are no actions held by God that are wasted.

This verse alone is one of my favorite verses in the Bible. However, its meaning can only be interpreted to its fullest based upon the faith of the reader. One of little faith, like Peter, will panic in times of uncertainty. One of great faith however, will always come back to this verse and remember there is light at the end of every tunnel.

There will be many times in life where we face a rough patch. We may face a week ahead of us full of long work days. We may come to a time where we are not getting along with our family very well. Not to say these are not tough, because they are, but these are all temporary life moments. These storms are nothing compared to living with cancer for ten years or losing a loved one at a young age. These storms have permanent effects and can alter one's emotional state of being, but it doesn't have to define it. There is nothing wrong with being angry in a moment of uncertainty, but if we let it define our actions and mindset is when it takes a toll on our life for good.

A rough patch I have personally watched and observed is about my Mom.

Let me start this section off by saying I truly have the best Mom on the planet. She always puts Dad, David and me before herself. While she knew she was in the midst of a storm every single day, she still led with a loving, caring heart.

During February of my freshman year, my mom began to experience severe pain in her stomach- daily. She lost a good amount of weight and would spend everyday aching in pain. And when she went to the doctor, nothing was diagnosed. There was no explanation for what was going on.

She began to see multiple doctors and specialists, and they finally stumbled upon something they were familiar with. She was diagnosed with Crohn's disease, which is an inflammatory disease of the digestive tract. While they began to give medication, the symptoms would not go away.

Most adults take a test when they are around 50 years old to check for colon cancer, called a colonoscopy. Because of the ongoing symptoms, the doctors scheduled one for my mom at age 46. Quite a turn of events going from a possible disease to a test for cancer.

I wish I could say now that the test was fine, but in reality it took a turn for the worse. My mom was told she had a cancerous polyp in her colon.

At that time, anxiety began to grow in her mind. She started to worry about the future and questioned why things were happening in the present. She was in a tough spot.

Along with the ongoing tests for the cancer, my mom endured more tests to dig deeper into why she had her stomach problems. She continued the treatment for Crohn's and it was not helping. She lost 44 pounds in 10 months and the symptoms were not going anywhere. What was going on?

After many tests and talks with the doctors, my mom was told she in fact did not have Crohn's, but IBS (Irritable Bowel Syndrome) and would need a different treatment. While IBS is still tough, it is not as bad as Crohn's. My mom was finally excited about some positive news.

Let's take a look back at the order of events. My mom was alarmed by the pain in her stomach and was sent to the doctor. They gave her a test four years prematurely, and found an unexpected cancer hiding in her colon.

If she had not gone to the doctor originally for her pain, the cancer would have sat in her colon four additional years.

It was a sign. One thing led to the next. There was a reason why she needed to get to the doctor that day. And because she listened to that feeling, doctors were able to attack the cancer early and quickly.

To this day, my mom is cancer free.

Yes, she has to watch what she eats. Yes, she has pain on some days. But my mom is happy. She went from the world turning on her to a peaceful state of being. The original path seemed uncertain and very bumpy, but her final destination was peace.

My mom is super grateful and super humble. What happened was far beyond what she could have imagined, and never would she have thought to this day she would be healthy again.

She had her moments of confusion. There were times she was angry and questioned God. But in the end, she realized

His plan is far more knowledgeable than we can ever imagine. She trusted Him, because she knows He loves her.

My mom's storm was calmed. Her situation worked for the good. She showed me so many things during the process, such as patience, perseverance, and kindness.

I remember reading this verse to her when things took a turn:

"For I consider that the sufferings of this present time are not worth comparing to the glory that is going to be revealed to us." Romans 8:18

Your suffering is no match for God's power. His glory is far superior to Satan's tricks! When problems arise and you have lost all hope, remember there's a God who promises peace. It's only a matter of trust.

Life Will Throw Curveballs

Throughout our lives, we will face many challenges and setbacks. Something that we must make sure of is to not let those setbacks define who we are. How do we do this? By not giving in to the world and it's temptations. Turning to God and asking Him to lead is always smart, but running away from Him and losing strength is not. One of my favorite verses about that is Romans 12:2. It reads,

"And do not be conformed to this world, but be transformed by the renewing of your mind, that you may prove what is that good and acceptable and perfect will of God."

Running from God and running to the world will only dig you deeper into a hole. Running to the world consists of chasing money, fame, drugs, alcohol, sexual desires, etc. The common thing between all of these temptations is that they are all so *temporary,* but may have long lasting effects. Mark 8:36 says:

"For what will it profit a man, if he gains the whole world, and loses his own soul?"

This verse speaks volumes to me. If we really think about it, nothing in this world can satisfy our needs. If you become a millionaire, there will be a want for more money. If you become famous, there will be a want for more followers on social media. If you become addicted to a drug, there will be a want for more drugs. If it satisfied you, there would never be a desire for more. However the one thing that can satisfy you is God's grace, and that is most definitely needed. We will never need more grace because God has already given it to us-abundantly. His never ending grace is a gift.

When life does get tough, it is completely normal to feel empty and in need of help. We may feel like our current situation is just too much to handle. We may be full of anxiety because of a lost loved one. But the answer is not to go run wild into the world. The answer is to run directly to God and give Him all of your cares.

You may be saying it is not that easy. And frankly it's not easy, it's really hard. But in the whole scheme of things, God has already won your battles. The ultimate battle, eternal life has been won through Jesus. The world will throw distractions at you left and right, but if you keep your eyes on God and His promises, He will lead you through every storm. He promises He has a plan for you and your life if you trust Him. Going down our own paths of wants is not trusting Him. Asking Him for guidance and then making decisions accordingly though, is trust.

Our Inner Battles

Sin will always be a part of this world and a part of our make up. When Adam and Eve chose to bite into that apple, it set the foundation for all of man to become sinful. This was the first example ever of a temptation.

Every single day we will face a temptation. I'll say it again. Every single day that we live on this earth, we will face a temptation. Whether it be lust, pride, greed, or even something so small as eating a dessert we know we shouldn't be having, we will face temptations. Because we are sinful, we are all very vulnerable to fall into these temptations.

As Christians, it is our job to do our best in not falling short of these tests. We are called to live like Christ, and constantly giving in to the same temptation over and over again is not Christ-like. There must be some control on our behalf and some efforts in trying to resist Satan and his tests.

How do I do this? It is not an easy battle.

A lot of people always say to *fight* our temptations. Stay strong. Fight the urge. Defeat Satan.

This is not the best way to deal with them. The Bible tells us that the only way we will defeat Satan and his tests are to *flee* them. 2 Timothy 2:22 reads:

"Flee also youthful lusts; but pursue righteousness, faith, love, peace with those who call on the Lord out of a pure heart."

We can compare fighting temptations to a war. If we continue to fight our battles with a temptation, we will steadily be involved in the war. However if we flee from battle and leave the fight altogether, by default we will have no association with that war. There is no way we can still be involved in the war if we have left it altogether.

You may be thinking something like, "Isn't running away from something the cowardly thing to do?" Actually, running from sin is the courageous thing to do. It takes a lot to step out and say, "I am not going back to those old ways." If we choose to fight sin and continue our involvement, we are actually in fear of what may happen if we leave. There is fear of consequences, repercussions, cravings, whatever it may be. But the truth is, defeating Satan will never happen if we continue to fight him. He is too powerful for us. The way we beat Satan is to leave and resist him altogether so he has no hold on our lives any longer.

Fighting a temptation is a thing because deep down inside, we are wounded. There is a hole in us we are constantly trying to fill, thinking that the world can fulfill our needs.

It's important to remember that there is no need to fight in this war because Jesus has already won it. We are able to flee the fight altogether because Jesus beat death on the cross. His grace covers over any sin we have.

Because of Jesus, even when we fall short, we can be confident that He will remain loving. Although we don't want to recklessly commit the same sin over and over again, there is no need to feel a cloud of guilt or shame. There is someone much bigger than this world. He has already conquered sin and death. He promises never ending love to everyone. You are never too far gone.

A great example of this was when Jesus hung from the cross at Calvary. He hung there with two crooks, one on each side. While one crook mocked and cursed him, the other one humbled himself and acknowledged Jesus as the Son of God. When he asked Jesus to remember him when he came into the kingdom, Jesus then said to him, "Today you will be with me in paradise."

Our past mistakes do not define our future choices. Our present choices dictate our future decisions. We are never too far from Jesus. But we do need to make a conscious effort to flee temptation. If we guard our hearts from any outside teaser or test, we can assure ourselves we will not fall victim anymore. Now don't get me wrong, we are still human. By nature we will always be sinners who have fallen short of God's glory, but we can control our efforts in fleeing sin. Let Christ lead your heart and mind, and the same struggles you once had will become much easier to take on. When we keep our eyes on Him, we are reminded that we are more than conquerors in Christ.

Chapter 4: Faith Talks

"In every encounter we either give life or drain it; there is no neutral exchange." **-TobyMac**

There are so many people in this world. We see so many different faces and personalities and each one of them has their own story. Scientists say we see three million faces in our lifetime, while only remembering three thousand. What kind of impact do we have on each person?

Read again that quote at the beginning of the chapter. When we come into contact with someone, we have a choice to either leave a negative or positive impact. We have a choice to not let our bad day affect someone else's. We have a choice to change someone's life.

I'll give you an example. Let's say you had a stressful day at work. Your boss yelled at you for an idea you shared with the group, then you saw your lazy colleague get promoted when you had been working hard. You are the one who put in long nights, stayed way past your work hours, and lost sleep over trying to promote this idea. And somehow "that" guy is getting promoted.

On the way home, you stop at a McDonalds to get yourself a drink. You put in your order and when you drive up to the window, not only is it the wrong drink, but they spill it all over your lap in the handoff. Tough.

You are pissed. You start yelling at the worker for how clumsy they are. Your day was already bad earlier, and now this. Whoop-de-doo.

Little did you know, this worker had just been kicked out of the house by her family. She failed her college semester and got kicked out of school, leaving her with nothing to do and nowhere to live. Her parents were so ashamed they told her to just leave. So she went to her job to make some money.

She makes a small mistake, and now because your day wasn't how you wanted it to be, her day is worse. Her day is ruined.

My mom always told me life will get hard. If it hasn't already, there will come a time where you will feel so low, there is no hope left. But you have to fight against it, get back up, and trust that God has a bigger plan for you. There is always more in store in His plan.

Our actions are what mends society together. If we choose to be sour, the people around us will be sour. If we don't get our way, and complain, the people around us will complain. If we have so much work to do and don't feel like getting it done, what is telling someone else about it going to do? They are going to want to quit too!

These are some things we all catch ourselves complaining about some days:

I don't want to go to school.

I don't want to go to practice.

I don't feel like cutting my grandma's grass.

I don't feel like staying in the house all day.

I don't want to eat this food. I don't like it.

Talk about perspective. There are kids in hospitals right now wishing they could be out running on a field. There are families in foreign countries that have nowhere to live, that would love to be in a house. There are kids who have never been to school because they can't pay for it.

There are people with cancer. Battling for their lives.

And we are complaining about getting out of bed in the morning.

We have a choice every single day. We can be negative, Debbie-downers, who drain positivity out of people; or we can be optimistic and full of hope. Imagine if we spoke life to everyone we saw. The world would change drastically!

In the Bible, Jesus wants us to be as influential and positive as we can. He describes our lives like this: "But whoever causes one of these little ones who believe in Me to stumble, it would be better for him if a millstone were hung around his neck, and he were thrown into the sea" (Mark 9:42). While this may be severe and graphic, it is so true! What good is our lives if we sit around and wait for things to come our way. What good are we driving others *away* from Christ. Use your life as a light to others. Shine brightness on the people you meet.

Don't be a light bulb that doesn't turn on.

The Right Voice

Whether we realize it or not, who we hang around is who we become. It can be positive or negative, but over time our minds will follow what we see the most. 1 Corinthians 15:33 says, "Do not be misled: Bad company corrupts good character."

One of the most important jobs we have as a maturing individual is choosing the right friend group. If we surround ourselves with God-fearing hearts that thirst for righteousness, we will also grow to want to feel God. On the other hand, if we surround ourselves with liars, cheaters, and complainers, we will grow to lie, cheat, and complain. It's that simple.

As followers of Christ, it is our job not only to specify in the hearts we want to be around, but also *lead* them. We still have a choice to mandate action and motives of others. If we constantly lead with a loving heart, in turn we will grow love around us.

Think back to the kids we saw in Puerto Rico. For the hour or two that we visited them, we gave them our all. Yes we just traveled early in the morning a day before, yes we were crammed inside a bus all day, but that's nothing compared to what those children endured their whole lives. Our window for opportunity was so small but our lasting impact was so big-because we chose to live selflessly.

Something I tend to always fall back on is the Gospel story. It always reminds me to keep things in perspective. How can I complain, if the life I live is already a free gift?

What I mean by this is that Jesus came to save you and me. While we were yet sinners, Christ still died for us (Romans 5:8). We were born into sin and deserve the Fall. We have turned against God and journeyed down our own paths. But God *still* loves. He still sent His Son to die for us so that we may accept eternal life. If you look at it from this standpoint, we have no reason to complain about our lives. Through it all-the God of the universe still loves you and knows you by name. Boy is that an assuring thought!

While we have a choice to dictate what kind of people we operate with, it's also important to remember our actions are being watched by others too. Even though I surround myself with good hearts, what is my heart like? Am I being a good influence to my peers or am I worried about someone else? Our actions and words matter.

I can remember one time in grade school I was sitting with some friends at lunch. I was kind of in a bad mood because one of my good friends was not hanging out with me as much as he used to. He would spend more time with this girl he liked.

When we all sat down, I started thinking about what I could say to him that would convey the point of, "I want to hang out with you more man!" I couldn't think what to say, so I started getting mad. I began to call him names and say things that put him down, and everyone started laughing at him. I actually made him cry.

Why did my feelings become angry? I was being selfish. I began to envy the girl who was spending more time with him than me. I was thinking for myself instead of thinking about my friend's happiness. In turn, my response was fear and anger, instead of love. The loving thing would have been to just simply talk to him about it, but instead I reacted with my emotions. I feel bad about it to this day.

While we made up afterwards and are still friends now, that was a moment in my life I can clearly remember bringing down my peers. I was so caught up in my own feelings that his feelings did not even matter to me. When moments arise like that, it is important to take a breath and think about our actions before we make them.

That leads me to another point. He was my friend. Because we were so close, I had no problem reacting out of anger. I was comfortable with showing my stripes. But would I have done that to a complete stranger?

Sometimes we treat strangers better than the people we are closest to. Why? We want our only impression on those people to be positive. During that quick interaction, we choose love only to impress them. But reality is, choosing love should always be the answer, no matter who you are speaking with.

Your friends look up to you; that's why they are your friends. They see something in you they admire and want to emulate. So when we decide to act in anger or put them down, imagine the feelings they get. Someone they admire is telling them how bad they are! Not a good feeling, I'm sure. Love others out of the goodness of your heart. Don't try to put on a show or impress. Your actions will show how much you actually care.

Exceed Expectations

On August 3, 1981, Rebecca Shehane was born into the world. At the time, her parents Ronnie and Angie had already birthed two kids, but during this go around there were complications. Rebecca had Down syndrome.

During the time period of her birth, doctors recommended institutionalizing people with Down syndrome. This meant that they would be put into institutions and taken care of because of their condition. But Ronnie and Angie said, "No way!" They anxiously started down their journey.

At the time, they were both in shock. Having a child with Down syndrome was far from normal, and frankly they began to worry. They found themselves asking, "What do we do? Why do we have the burden of raising this child?" Fear began to form inside of them. Doubt started defining their actions. Their lives would change forever.

Throughout our lives, there will be times where God gives us something we question. We think that what is brought upon us will change our lives negatively. Because fear tempts us, the only way to fight it is with courage and faith. Even though I am hurt and even though this doesn't seem fair, I am going to trust that God knows what He is doing. He is the Creator of the universe! He knows our past, prepares us in the present, and will continue to use us to glorify Him in our future.

Faith and fear cannot exist together. If we say we have faith in God but worry about our current situations, what good is our faith? Isaiah 41:13 says, "For I am the LORD your God who takes hold of your right hand and says to you, Do not fear; I will help you." If we truly rely on our faith, we will understand that no matter how bad the situation may seem, the end product will always be good.

After a few months, Angie and Ronnie grew to accept and love their journey with Rebecca. They understood that Rebecca's life was a gift from God and was to be used to its fullest potential. Early on, she began to bring life to every room she entered. Angie developed a deep love for Rebecca and her needs. To this day, Angie volunteers in the Special Needs community and changes lives every day.

In 2003, Rebecca decided she wanted to be involved in the Special Olympics. She participated in bowling, swimming, bocce, and basketball at the Special Olympics Games in her home state of Georgia. Throughout the years she continued to improve her game, but more importantly continued to develop relationships with people. Rebecca met hundreds of new people and made so many new friends because of the Special Olympics.

Rebecca was not always a participant in swimming. She decided in 2016 that she wanted to try it out for the Games in May of the following year. She trained all winter with her new coach and she was more than ready to compete.

However when the race started, Angie noticed Rebecca was not going as fast as she could. Rebecca stayed right next to the person in the lane beside her- the whole race. Not once would she pass her fellow competitor; she stuck with them from the beginning to the end.

To Rebecca, it didn't matter what place she came in. She couldn't care less about receiving a medal. Rebecca just wanted to have fun and make the people around her happy. In turn, this put a smile on her face. She enjoyed celebrating with her friends after the meet, laughing and jumping around with excitement.

Although Rebecca still won a medal after the race, all eyes were centered on her big, beautiful smile. She understands that no matter what happens, the effect on those around you is most important. The accolades and accomplishments will come and go, but relationships last forever. She always cares for the people around her.

Rebecca is my aunt.

Rebecca has truly changed my life. She is the most positive, joyful, loving soul you will find on the face of this planet. She never complains about a situation and always sees the good in everything. Her laugh will never fail to put a smile on my face.

I can recall one time she came to one of my games. It wasn't the best game for me, but she couldn't care less. After the game I can remember going up to her and giving her a big hug while she told me, "Great job Ryan!" At that moment, my day was changed. Her love reminded me it is never about what we accomplish, but what we do for others.

Rebecca lives everyday out of love. She never gives an attitude if someone makes a mistake, or never scolds someone for messing something up. She forgives and she forgets. Imagine if the whole world lived like this! We all have a choice to show compassion to those around us. We all can choose to support one another in their race, or we can leave them out to dry. We can choose to care more about our relationships with people, or we can focus on nothing but ourselves.

To this day, everyone in the family knows that Rebecca is always someone you can count on. She will never leave you and always support you through it all. Just like all of us, her life is a gift. She is no different. While she may have Down syndrome, her attitude and determination never cease to limit her impact on others.

God, help me to choose to live selflessly and put others before me, just as Jesus did.

Amen.

Pride

Everyday after school I take the same road home, and everyday I see the same guy sitting out on the corner, holding a sign that says "Hungry." He is homeless.

Oftentimes, when we see homeless people on the street, our first few impressions are negative ones. We see these people as dirty, scary and even consider them failures. We anxiously wait for the light to turn green so we can zip by without any uncomfortable interactions.

One time after school, I was the one sitting right at the corner waiting for the light to turn green. As he started his usual walk down the line of cars, I rolled my window down and stopped him. I said, "What's up man!" He was shocked that someone actually took the time to talk to him. We had a very brief conversation and then I gave him my sandwich I had packed for myself. The light turned green and I drove off.

We have a choice to show love to everyone. Any time we have an interaction with someone, we have the opportunity to either make or break their day. Our words hold so much significance and value.

God sees each and every one of us the same. Whether we're a faith leader at church or a crook locked in prison, God sees only one thing- we are His children. Jesus didn't choose who He wanted to save on the cross, so we shouldn't choose who we show our love to! Everywhere you go, start by spreading faith, hope, and love. You never know what kind of impact you can have on someone that day.

A Daily Spark

A lot of times we find ourselves wondering how we can impact lives, every single day. It's hard having the time to reach out and talk to someone in need. So how can I do it?

Something I tried back in 2018 was group chats that included devotionals. I figured everyday if I sent out a verse to these people, they could find a reason to smile no matter how their day went. After putting it out there for people to join, I had a group chat of about 10 people.

Sweet, right? An easy way to spread God daily. I figured this was great. God was using me to speak to the hearts of others.

Until God told me He wasn't done. Over the years, more and more people asked to get into this group chat. Numbers were piling up and I had to create new ones for new people. Everyday, I was getting the opportunity to share Jesus with people who needed Him most. To this day, more than 150 people are receiving verses through these group chats.

The cool thing for me is that each one of these chats has its own uniqueness. Not only are there people of different color and genders, but each chat has individuals from around the country. God has brought me so many places in my life to meet so many different people. From teammates I played a single game with to life long friends, they are in there. From coaches I have met along the way to respected adults I admire, they are in there. From school buddies to people I have met on social media, they are in there. God has found a way for me to share His good news, even to people I don't see everyday. That's incredible!

Think back to how many faces you see in a lifetime. Now think about how many of those faces you have talked to about Jesus. If we make an effort to share God to everyone we meet, think about how different the world will be. Think about how many more lives Jesus will save! Think about the impact you will have on these hearts.

Ask God to show you where He wants to take you. Ask Him to use you! Once you open your heart to Him, there is no limit on how much He can accomplish.

God, help me to never be ashamed of your grace. Use me to help others see you. I'm stepping out of my comfort zone, and I'm ready to work for Your kingdom.

Amen.

A Shining Light

On February 12 of 2002, Noah Homayouni was born 8 weeks prematurely. After some time in the NICU, he was cleared to be taken home a couple weeks earlier than expected. Noah was a fighter. He was super competitive in everything he did and always put forth his best effort.

Growing up, Noah was taught to attend church and participated in Vacation Bible School. As he got older, it was difficult to make time for church, but Noah remained steadfast. He learned to choose his friends wisely, picking ones that would influence him for the better, not for the worse. He understood the repercussions of making bad choices, and wanted to stay focused on his life and future.

Noah was always doing things to keep busy. He was an athlete and loved to run, which led him to play lacrosse. He worked hard all the time at the game he loved. As a freshman, he earned a spot on varsity come playoff time.

During his sophomore year, the lacrosse team hired a new coach but Noah didn't really connect with him. After a few arguments and disagreements, Noah grew tired of the negative relationship with his coach. He talked to his mom about it.

His mother, Melissa, gave Noah some great advice. She asked him, "Have you ever prayed about it?" He said no, and she told him to pray when he was having self-doubt. Noah did so and his relationship with Christ grew stronger. He began to pray more and more. He prayed before every game.

Throughout lacrosse season, Noah continued to strive forward. He worked hard all summer, returning his junior year as a leader on the team. He continued to grow in his faith and was eager to learn more about Christ. Unbeknownst to me, he was added to one of the Bible verse group chats by a friend of mine.

Noah started to really understand his faith and grew to keep a good perspective. He understood that his purpose in life was more than his small accolades and dreams. He knew that when God said "no," there was a reason. Noah trusted God, to wait until He said "yes."

As senior year rolled around, Noah developed into a really good lacrosse player. He earned a scholarship to play at Howard Community College, but that didn't stop him from continuing to work hard. Noah filled out physically and was ready to dominate his senior year. Although he was confident in his abilities, he maintained a humble attitude which rubbed off on his teammates. When things got tough, he always saw the positive. Noah truly impacted those around him.

On March 12, the night of his first scrimmage, he received devastating news. During this time, the world was beginning its fight with the Coronavirus pandemic, and as a precaution they shut down all schools. Noah would not play his senior year. But he remained positive, continuing to work out, getting better at his sport and growing spiritually. He took no days off.

On April 2, Noah was outside of his house working out and shooting goals into his net. He suddenly heard gunshots from the house next door and saw a man running from the bushes. Noah was then shot and killed by this person, who eventually took his own life.

Noah had his life taken way too early. He was affected by something so fluke and random. He touched so many lives around him and brought life to everybody he encountered. He had grown to lead others and spread joy to those who needed it. His good spirit brought everyone together in his community. His journey was just getting started only to be stopped by an evil act.

Life is challenging. Noah did not deserve what happened. His family doesn't deserve to live without him. The world lost a special person. Why did this happen?

We all have sole purposes for our lives. God gives us all opportunities at certain moments to shine on others and impact their lives. While Noah's life was cut short, his time here was spent exactly how God intended it to be. Noah lived for others. He spread love. He gave others hope and motivated them not only to work hard, but to grow in Christ. Noah was truly a light in his community. I know God is so proud of him and is giving him a big hug right now. Noah was a soldier in the kingdom of God.

At some point, we are all going to pass from this world. It's inevitable. It's not easy to deal with the sorrow and pain that comes with losing a loved one. But something that can help is to trust God. He holds this world in His big hand. He knows exactly what is going on and will work all things for the good. Although we may not always see why He is doing something, we can trust there is reason and purpose behind it. Noah's story and life has brought so many together in love. While this may seem like a loss, God says look at all of the hearts won. Noah brought others to Christ. He knew that if his life was used for serving, he would be fine with whatever else happened.

Noah is looking down on all of us right now. We all can make a difference! No matter what happens, we can trust that our good works can make a change. When Noah sees his Mom in heaven, together they can say- *we made it*. While it may hurt now, let us remember we live forever in eternity. That's the power of the Gospel!

The Big 3

In 1 Corinthians 13:13, Paul says "And now abideth faith, hope, love, these three; but the greatest of these is love." We all have heard of these words, but what do they truly mean?

Faith

Faith is defined in the Bible as the substance of things hoped for, the evidence of things not seen (Hebrews 11). Faith is what connects us with God. We cannot physically see or touch God, so we must trust and believe in what He says. That is faith.

Our faith is what helps us persevere through our lives. In the Bible, God promises that all things will work for the good to those who love Him (Romans 8). If this is so, then no matter what happens, your life will always be guided by Him. There will be plenty of trials and tribulations in between, but a glorious final destination is promised. He doesn't promise it will be easy but He does promise He will be with you.

Something that challenges our faith is doubt and worry. When life throws a curveball and you are feeling uncertain, the natural tendency is to worry. We try to take things into our own hands and take control of the situation. But the truth is, the harder we try to control the uncontrollable, the more it will negatively impact us. Instead of getting trapped into the lie of control, choose to combat it with faith. Your faith trusts that the situation will not change what God is planning for your life, no matter what you may be facing. In Daniel 3, we are introduced to Shadrach, Meshach, and Abednego. These men were natives to Jerusalem. During that time, King Nebuchadnezzar conquered the land and became ruler. As the new leader, he made a golden idol to represent his power and demanded everyone bow down to it when instructed. But the three men denied the King and said they would not bow down to this idol because they only serve the One True King, Jesus.

Keep in mind that this story took place about 600 years before Jesus was born. Although nobody knew of Him yet, God had promised a Messiah that would save the world. These three men trusted in that promise and believed in His Word. Nebuchadnezzar had never heard of Jesus and could not get over the fact that they would not bow to his idol. He was so mad that he ordered them to be thrown into a scalding hot furnace. He even raised the temperature hotter than normal. Their last words before being thrown in were, "Our God will deliver us, but even if He doesn't, we will not bow to your idol, O King."

Shadrach, Meshach, and Abednego were thrown into the furnace. It was so hot you couldn't even see inside, and the soldiers guarding the furnace burned to death! As Nebuchadnezzar peaked inside, he saw that the three men were not burning. They stood tall and perfectly fine. He called for them to be taken out and later declared free worship to all citizens of the land. He was in awe.

The moral here is not that if you have faith, God promises He will provide. If this was the case there would be no need for faith, because everything would be freely given. These men stood strong against the flames and trusted God and His plan for them. They understood that whatever happened, His hand was working for the greater good. In the end, their lives were spared, and there would be no more idol worshipping. The lives of the people in the city were changed.

When we face trials in life, we have two choices. We can worry, lose trust, and try to run away from it, or we can stand tall and know that the God of the universe is on our side. Our faith is what holds us together and gives us confidence in our actions. When we take a step into the unknown, we should remind ourselves that God already knows what lies ahead. Having faith in our decisions will help eliminate our fear of the problems we face. Like the three men, even the fire we face cannot separate us from God's love.

Hope

Our hope can be defined as the confidence we have that God will deliver us. The Bible teaches us that Jesus will indeed return and all of His people will go to heaven. We can live in hope by reminding ourselves daily that God has not forsaken us.

Hope and faith relate to each other because both are trusting what we have not yet seen. If our faith is strong in Christ, then naturally we will have hope in Him throughout our lives. While faith is trusting in the plans we have not yet seen, hope is being confident that at some point, God will glorify what He has in store for you. Hope keeps us calm at our darkest, most stressful points.

Let us recall the story of David and Goliath. Israel was set to go to war with the Philistines, who had a secret weapon. Everyday of the war, the over 9-foot tall Goliath would go to the front of the army and mock the Israelites. While King

Saul, their leader, wanted to fight back, they physically had no chance at taking down the mighty Goliath.

Then the young David burst onto the scene. David watched how Goliath mocked and disrespected his fellow people, so he vowed to take him down. After he talked to King Saul, he went to face Goliath with no armor, a sling and five stones. But what the people didn't know was that David had a secret weapon of his own… hope.

David was confident that God would guide and take care of him during this battle. He knew that God promised to provide strength and to be faithful. While David may have been facing a giant, he had a much bigger giant of his own in his heart.

David walked up to Goliath with his sling and stones, and watched as he mocked the Israelites one last time. He said, "I come in the name of the Lord Almighty, the God of Israel." After watching Goliath laugh at his remarks, David slung one of his stones and hit Goliath right in the head, knocking him to his knees. David then grabbed Goliath's sword and pierced his chest, ending the torment of this giant. If David had not trusted God here, that puny stone would have done nothing to Goliath. But because he had confidence in God's power, the impossible happened. David was victorious.

We will all face giants in our lives that may seem too big to be conquered. The problems we face may seem too tough to overcome. But with faith and hope in God's promises, we can overcome any trial or tribulation.

It is much easier to understand when you look at it like this. God is sovereign and rules over all. He created everything and knows everything; we know this from the Bible. God also promises to lead each and every one of us. The small problems we face can never change God's path for us, because He has already shaped it. No matter what comes our way, He won't let go and will not change your course. Your glorified end is still coming and your prosperous being is still alive. That is hope. Trusting that through the hardships, Jesus Christ has a special plan for us to prosper.

Love

Love is the final virtue I will discuss in this section, and frankly it is the most important. There are so many things I can talk about that relate to love. It is a wide emotion that holds so much meaning, but is interpreted differently by each individual.

The Biblical definition of love is, "Putting others before yourself without expecting anything in return." True love is shown when things go wrong. But, society has changed that point of view. Today most of us see love as a relationship based feeling, instead of a way we treat everyone. We are told to love one another, no matter who they are (John 15).

Love is not a feeling- it is a choice. When we look at love as a feeling, we are living for our own satisfaction. Instead of choosing others before ourselves out of love, we are choosing ourselves over others out of fear. Love cannot be a feeling we get because feelings are temporary. Feelings will only get you so far. But when we choose love, we are letting love define our choices and existence. Focusing too much on feelings will misconstrue the true meaning of love.

Now I'm not saying feeling love is not ordinary, and not ok. Feelings usually are created when showing love, but when the relationship is based on feelings things start to awry. When we choose to love as a choice, we naturally will feel love for that person, whereas if we love for the feeling, those feelings will quickly fade and the love will end. In that case, the love was never genuine.

Jesus is the perfect example of love. John 15:13 says,

"Greater love has no one than this, than to lay down one's life for his friends."

While we are yet sinners, Christ still died for us. I'm sure Jesus didn't feel love at the time while He was on the cross. But He chose love for you and me and did so through His actions. Instead of seeking love for Himself as a feeling, He gave love to all of us as a choice.

If you read the Bible, you will learn that the opposite of love is actually fear. Every choice we make is out of love or fear. There is no other choice. Whether that fear may be our ego, pride, selfishness, or the like, fear still rules that decision. But if you make decisions out of love, naturally you will be ruled by selflessness, compassion, and kindness.

When all we seek is the feeling of love, fear is ruling that decision. We fear of losing that love, or being betrayed, or having something taken from us. But when love is a choice, we understand that no matter what the world may do, our love will remain constant. We must stand strong in our choice of love because once we choose fear, over time fear will define us. We do not want fear to define our choices and dictate our motives. To combat that simply choose love. Those choices you are making in fear because of your pride, choose love and practice humility. 1 John 4:18 says,

*"There is no fear in love; but perfect love casts out fear;
because fear involves torment. But he who fears has not been
made perfect in love."*

Now you may be asking yourself, how do I choose love for
people who constantly act in fear? The answer is simple. Let
your love outweigh any fearful decision they make. When you
are dealing with someone who is fearful, the answer is to stop
feeding them fear. Instead, feed them love. Over time, our
love will start to fight their fear. When they choose to put you
down, raise them up. When they choose selfishness, you
choose selflessness. When anger rises in their hearts, combat
that with peace and gratitude.

Sometimes we try to take back things we have lost from
fearful people. When we attempt to get back what was taken
from us, we actually cut off our own source of love altogether-
God. The people who hurt us cannot mend us back together,
neither can we mend ourselves back together. This is fear now
defining our lives. We fear losing something we had forever,
and in turn cut off our love for others, and love for God. God
is love. To choose fear is to lose trust in God and disregard
His promises to provide. Instead of trying to gain back what
we have lost, remember we have a source that will forever
produce.

When moments of fear begin to rise, remember the story of
Jesus. He chose love for all of us in a situation where He could
have easily chosen not to. Instead of putting Himself first, He
put everyone else first while on that cross. He knew the
gruesome death He would have to endure. He also knew that
in that moment, if He made a fearful decision it would forever
doom all of creation. We would have no chance at eternal life.

But our loving decisions have greater purposes. Jesus choosing love there and enduring our pain now gives us a chance to live forever in Heaven.

Our lives are not about us. Choosing love puts others first, while choosing fear is all about us. Love sees life from the outside, while fear sees life from the inside. If the decision will benefit you in the present but have short term impact, that is a fearful decision. However if the decision hurts you now but has long term impact, that is a loving decision.

Believe, When No One Else Does

Life is tough. We will all come to a point where we face a giant in front of us, and we have two choices. We can either back down and stay down, or find a way to get back up. Choosing to believe that there is good in the midst of the bad is the first step in overcoming these obstacles. We can all believe that God has the power to change our darkness to light.

The key to overcoming these bumps in the road is based on our faith. We must realize that on our own, we are capable of so little. But with Christ, we are capable of moving mountains. When attempting things on our own, we see only what we want to happen. We forget about the truth, putting others first and trusting God in our hardships. We lose sight of the moment.

But when we believe in Christ, our hearts are open to anything and everything that we see. We trade selfishness for selflessness. We see others before we see ourselves. Ultimately we put our situation in God's hands, and with Him leading there is nothing we can't do.

Why can we believe in the middle of a catastrophe? In reality, even in the midst of a storm, we will be ok. There is still a God who knows what He is doing. There is still a God who loves you and calls you His child. There is still a God who wants eternity with *you*. In that case, we have no reason not to believe. The temporary storms we endure now have no match for the eternal glory we will soon see.

Our actions matter. We dictate our attitude towards everything, whether things go our way or not. Our positivity can influence the people around us. When we choose to believe, no matter the circumstance, the people around you will believe and everyone will work as one.

Positivity is contagious. Be the person people look to in a crisis. Be the person people rely on and trust to bring hope. This world needs leading, and the first step is to believe in each other, and believe in Christ. As one we can do so little, but together nothing is out of reach. Besides, we are already more than conquerors through Christ.

"And Jesus looking upon them said to them, wth men this is impossible; but with God all things are possible." Matthew 19:26

"I can do all things through Christ who strengthens me." Philippians 4:13

Chapter 5: Virtues of Love, Virtues of Fear

"God loves each of us as if there were only one of us." - **Augustine**

To dig deeper into love, we have the 7 virtues of what love is: patience, kindness, truthfulness, protection, trust, hope, and perseverance. We are also given the 7 virtues of fear: anger, rudeness, envy, pride, unforgiveness, boastfulness, and selfishness.

Patience

Patience is being able to see the good in something, even when we are angry or uncertain. It's easy to be patient and happy when life is going well, but what happens when life takes a turn for the worse? What happens when something doesn't go our way?

The answer is actually gratitude. We have no right to get mad at someone who has wronged us and made us lose our patience. Why? Because Jesus, the Son of God, has not done that to you and me. Jesus continues to love us and look for the best in our hearts. If He didn't, we would have no shot at eternal salvation.

Patience can also relate to anxieties in your life. You may be anxious about a job opportunity, a test grade, or even a marriage proposal, but if we are not patient then we will act out of fear; fear of the unknown and uncertainty of what may happen when we wait. But the truth is, when we trust in God's promises, we understand that all things will be made for the good, no matter the situation. He has your life covered in its entirety.

On the other hand, fear tells us instead of patience we choose anger. We get angry at the results we don't see, outcomes we don't want or things we don't want to do. Choosing anger is actually being fearful, and frankly you're getting angry at God. God rules all, so when things aren't going right we tend to ask Him, "what in the world are you doing?"

Anger with God is thinking we know more than God. We get angry because we think what is happening now will hurt or limit us. Things are not going the way *we* see them. But the truth is, God doesn't see things our way- He can't. We see things temporally, while God is all-knowing. He knows exactly when to come in and save the day. It's up to us how much we trust Him, and how patient we really are.

Kindness

Kindness is when we choose to act in the best interest of others, even if it hurts right now. We all can be nice to people when things are easy, but what happens when you have to make a difficult decision for someone? What happens if you must hold your teammate accountable during a workout? Kindness is what pushes us to push others. The selfish thing to do would be to not say anything and allow our friend to continue limiting themselves.

If we are not careful, we will choose to be rude instead of kind. While a kind heart is constantly looking out for others, a rude heart is turning others away. Being rude is not just saying something mean or having an attitude with someone you don't like. Being rude is having no care or respect for someone, and that simply is unjust. Jesus tells us to love everyone, not bring them down. Being rude is acting in fear.

If we choose to be rude, we are fearful of two things. We use our rudeness to put that person down, not allowing our ego to be demoralized. We also think we are better than that person and can love them less. But the truth is, we are called to treat everyone the same. Kindness to all people is what will cast out all rudeness, and lead to more loving decisions instead of fearful ones.

This is especially relevant when we talk about our "make or break" moments with people. In that quick second we have with someone, choosing rudeness will drain life, but choosing kindness will speak it. We never want to recall moments where the one interaction we had with someone was negatively impactful.

This leads me to another point: the platforms we are given can determine what lasting impact we have on others through our interactions. By this I mean that our level of influence factors into how much people really care about our attitudes. If you encounter some random guy at a gas station that accidentally bumps into you and doesn't say sorry, you probably would not be overly offended. On the other hand if that man was the President of the United States, you would probably freak out and rant about how rude he was. If we are given a platform to excel on, it is extremely important to bring love and kindness to those people we meet. Choosing fear and rudeness will not only hurt you, but hurt them in the long run. These people came to you because they look up to you.

I'll give you an example. When we were kids, David and I were obsessed with watching professional wrestling. We bought a bunch of action figures and accessories and we would play all day with those things. Finally one of their shows came to Washington D.C. and we had to go. When we got there, the place was sold out.

Throughout the night, as the wrestlers finished their match, they would exit the ring to the left and file backstage through this passage on the side. It just so happened that our seats were right at the end of that side.

About halfway through the show, our favorite wrestler came out to compete in his match. I honestly do not remember if he won or lost. But I do remember seeing him begin to walk down that long passage to get backstage. As he walked past us my dad shouted, "Hey man you are the best!"

He didn't even glance at us.

Now look, I'm sure talking to thousands of fans every single night gets tiring. He may have even just lost the match, I don't remember. But that interaction has stuck with us since it happened. I don't remember much from that entire night except that exact moment. To this day, our family recalls that moment and our opinion of that wrestler has forever changed.

In this case, his platform was professional wrestling. Kids of all ages look up to this guy. He had a shot to show love to a young kid like me, but instead he chose fear. It could have been fear of his pride or his ego, I'm not sure. But because of his platform, I remember that more than any other interaction with someone who isn't as "famous."

Kindness and love will always conquer rudeness and defeat. When situations arise and we have a choice between these two, let's always choose to be kind. Our lives are about our impact on others, and it starts with our words and actions.

Truthfulness

Love is truthful in many ways. While a lot of us may believe being truthful is just not lying, truth goes way beyond that. Truth seeks the good and reasoning behind every choice people make. Instead of assuming the worst, truth allows for complete explaining and understanding. If we choose to act in fear, we will act in anger of the situation without finding the true reasoning behind the action.

When dealing with misunderstandings with other people, it is important we seek the truth behind their action before we react out of anger or fear. Most of the time, one makes a hurtful decision because they are struggling with something themselves. Instead of adding to the fire and causing strife, love provides care for that person. It takes courage to put your pride aside and seek the truth about the other person.

Speaking of pride, the fearful choice in this situation is just that. Pride blocks off our hearts to other hearts because we are afraid of our ego being torn down. Instead of looking out for the other person, we are so focused on our self dignity that we ignore them. Pride is really our outer appearance attempting to be strong, but on the inside we are hurt. This problem can be resolved if we simply seek the truth, and most of the time, the hurtful decision someone made was unintentional.

When we put our pride aside, we put others first. We understand their side of the story before we react to ours. The loving thing to do is to seek truth and provide assistance, instead of beating them down to the ground. It will take some courage along with some humility, but you will see in the long run it will benefit both hearts tremendously.

Jesus is a perfect example of loving through truth. If He looked at the sin in each one of us, we would be nothing. We would be defined as sinners and would have no hope. However Jesus looks at us by our hearts. His love for us seeks the truth in our decisions and focuses more on the why, than the what. Jesus puts all of us first before Himself, and because of that we all have a chance at eternal life. Boy am I glad He looks out for me more than He looks out for Himself.

When tensions arise and we have a choice between love or fear, choose love and seek the truth. Put your pride aside and put the other person first. God says that in His eternal kingdom, the last shall be first and the first shall be last.

Protection

Protection in love is more than being a personal bodyguard for someone. Telling others what they really need to hear instead of what they may want to hear is protecting them. When telling them what they want to hear, we are hiding the truth from them and beginning a long journey of misunderstanding in their hearts. We think that the loving thing to do is to make them feel good with false information, when in reality it's selfish on our part. We fear the unknown of the future and because we worry, we attempt to cover up all possible negative effects. Instead of giving them reality, we give them fantasy and keep them in their fearful, selfish states of being.

However, we must make sure what we are telling them will strengthen them instead of causing more worry and anxiety. Obviously there are some cases where people really do not need to hear something, and doing so will bring unneeded stress upon them. Our words must be uplifting and supportive instead of combative and negative. If we are telling them something just to say it for our benefit, we are not really protecting them.

Envy is the fearful way to act in this case and will only bring selfishness. When we become jealous we tend to make choices that only benefit ourselves and hurt others, which puts us above everyone else. It is very important to think about our words before we say them to people. Is what I'm saying truly going to help this person in the long run? Am I bringing them closer to God and keeping them away from evil? Am I saying this to make them feel bad about their decisions? When we refuse to let envy define our motives, in turn love will rule our lives and decisions.

Trust

When we love, we trust. When we fear, we do not trust. It's that simple. Love tells us to seek and believe in something while fear tells us to abandon it.

When things happen to us that bring uncertainty, the first thing we do is stop trusting. We close ourselves off from the outside world and leave people by themselves. But that is not loving. We cannot say we love someone but abandon them at the same time. Love fights selfishness and seeks understanding, even if we feel like we have been taken advantage of.

I'm not saying when people are trying to walk all over us to just allow them. Constant pain and abuse is only hurting you and hurting themselves. We must love them enough to walk away and trust that our impressions on them can change their heart. Allowing them to continually make fearful decisions is selfish on our part because we do not trust what the future holds.

Losing trust in God is the last thing we want to do. When we walk away from God's love and His promises, we abandon the path He has started us on. In turn we will journey down our own paths of uncertainty, which most likely will end in pain or even more worry. However, if we stay connected to God's promises, we can trust Him saying that He will guide and provide for us. Loving God consists of trusting and following Him. That is the basis of our faith.

Unlike trust, unforgiveness is acting in fear. We begin to doubt and question the source instead of seeking truth and believing in what is said. Failing to forgive others only leads to our own destruction and over time will corrupt our hearts. We will no longer seek the good in people and instead seek the bad. We will no longer love from our hearts, but begin to love just to say we love.

Jesus is the greatest example of forgiveness. While we all fail Him every single day, He continues to seek the good in our hearts. He continues to forgive and to provide. If the Son of God can forgive and trust our hearts, what makes us think we cannot forgive and trust our friends?

Trust will always defeat unforgiveness. Trusting someone else is not easy, but in love it is required. Trust allows us to seek the good in others, and love them truly because of our loving hearts. Unforgiveness guards our hearts from others and prohibits love to be shared.

Let's look at the story of Zechariah and Elizabeth. The Bible begins their story describing their state of life, without children. This couple had become "old and childless," and had given up on having a child. They served God and honored Him their whole lives, but they really did want a child.

One day when Zechariah entered the temple, the angel Gabriel appeared to him with good news. He told Zechariah that God chose him and his wife to bear a son, and to name him John. But Zechariah knew his current state, and doubted the angel. In Luke 1, he acknowledged that he was an old man and his wife was well among her years. Because of his lack of faith, he immediately became mute. He lost his voice until the birth of his son many months later, where he ecstatically proclaimed, "His name is John!"

After he regained his voice, Zechariah immediately thanked God. He recalled how God promises He will provide as long as we trust. He thanked God for fulfilling His promises and praised Him for His redemption.

This story can be used to interpret our lives. The minute we lose trust in God, we will then lack something we used to have. Whether that be confidence, love for others, or selflessness, we will lose a piece of our old self. We will approach a long stretch where we feel abandoned, alone, and hopeless. But reality is, the only way we feel that way is because we are journeying down a never ending path by ourselves! When we trust God and His promises, we realize every path will have an expected end to prosper. Zechariah saw this when he saw the birth of his baby boy.

Loving through trust is one of the most important things we can do. Instead of thinking others will bring us down, let's focus on our part and conquer all disbelief by providing trust to bring others up.

Hope

Hope is one of my most favorite things to talk about. Having hope does not just mean you are always happy and positive. Hope is believing that no matter what, God will guide and provide for us. We can't have hope in ourselves simply because we can't control our future and life. Our hope comes from God. He holds what is in store for us and promises to lead us through. That is what gives us hope.

A verse so commonly known and used to bring hope is Romans 8:28. I have mentioned this verse already in a previous chapter but I truly think it conveys the point of hope more than anything else in the Bible.

"And we know that in all things God works for the good of those who love Him, who have been called according to His purpose." Romans 8:28

There are six key words in this verse that scream hope at us: all things work for the good (I bet you counted out all six words). How crazy is that! God promises everything to have an expected end. He loves us so much that however our lives end here on earth, He promises a destination of prosperity.

The truth is, the "good" that is being referred to is actually eternal life in heaven. We may think that good means winning the lottery, or getting a new job if we pray about it, or winning a championship after praying pregame. However the good God talks about is a promised life in heaven with Him. What more can we truly ask for than to live forever in eternity?

The small things we attain here on earth do not matter. The rough trials will come and go, but somehow we must find a way to fight back. When we remember our lives are held by the Creator of the universe, we realize that everything truly will work for the good. The pain may be excruciating right now, but soon you will find peace in the eternal life God promises to those who love Him.

Choosing hope is the result of loving the source. We hope in what the source brings because we know that love holds the relationship together.

Being boastful can lead to many fearful choices we don't want to make. You may be thinking, "How do boastfulness and hope relate enough to contradict each other?" The truth is, if we lose hope, we lose our foundation in the source and begin to project ourselves. We think that we can make things happen and bring good on our own. We project strength and power but truly, we have nothing.

Boastfulness is one of the most powerful things we can do to drain life. If we aren't careful, our pride and ego will rule our lives. Instead of living for others, we live to promote ourselves to others. This is selfish and ultimately fearful, because we are constantly looking for reassurance. We fear we are not as good as those we are talking to.

Boastfulness and confidence are different. Confidence tells us that we are more than enough through Christ, while boastfulness tells others we are maybe enough by ourselves. The glory shifts in this case. It's not about us. It's about God and others, and constant emphasis on our greatness only highlights us.

God already calls you His child. Jesus already loves you enough to die in your place. Who are you trying to impress? Let society think what they want about you from your actions and not your words. If you live selflessly and put others first, you won't feel the need to prove to anyone you're worth anything.

Perseverance

Perseverance is something I think we all should strive to do in our lives. Persevering in any action shows heart and takes courage. When we choose to persevere, we continue to fight forward no matter what. A loss cannot define our attitude. A setback cannot dictate our fight.

If we choose to live in fear of the unknown, perhaps we may never take that step in persevering. We won't have enough courage to keep trying again and again. In reality, this is being selfish and only looking out for ourselves. We fear of being embarrassed of ourselves or not being good enough, so we decide to quit altogether. But if we persevere in love, we are no longer in it for our own good- but for God and others. Our positive attitude rubs off on everyone else and our courage is seen by many. In turn we will see that we have more left in the tank than we ever thought we did.

Life is full of failures. There will be times where you are knocked down so hard, you may have no idea how to get up. You may go bankrupt. You may lose a loved one. You may get fired from a job you desperately needed. But it's not about how many times you get pushed down, it's how you respond and get back up.

I can recall a short story from the summer of 2017. At the time I was playing in Georgia for a tournament and was super pumped to get out in front of some colleges. While I was eager to be out on the field, apparently my bat was not feeling the same way. I could not find a hit in over 15 games.

I remember one night during this "slump," I was standing in the outfield during a game. I remember looking up at the sky and wondering, "Why is this happening?" I was getting more frustrated and angry as each day rolled by. Things were far from looking up.

Now in reality, this is such a *small* pothole in my road. Not getting a hit in a baseball game is not as big of a deal as hearing you are diagnosed with cancer. But it was tough for a 14-year old me. I had to figure out how to get myself on my feet and move on to the next opportunity. I had to fill my mind with positive thoughts and approach each day as a gift. And in time, I broke out with a smashing double up against the wall. The light at the end of the tunnel finally made its appearance.

Perseverance is important in many ways throughout our lives, but something we must persevere first and foremost in is love. The only way we will not see love is if we refuse to love. Love does not fail, but oftentimes we do fail to love. If we choose to seek the best in others over and over again, even if it may hurt, that is love. The selfish, fearful thing to do would be to abandon these people and avoid any type of pain towards yourself.

Why should we continue to persevere in love? Because that's what Jesus does for us… every single day. While we sin over and over again each day, He never fails to see the good in our hearts. Instead of calling us sinners (who we most definitely are), He calls us His children. If that is the case, then we have no reason to say we cannot persevere in love for others as well.

Now that we have discussed every virtue of love and fear, I want you to take a moment to reflect on each virtue. We have two choices in life when dealing with others, and that is to choose love or to choose fear. We can guard our hearts with selfishness, shoot pride in every direction, and envy those around us, or we can simply love. We can choose patience to those that may bring anger. We can be truthful to those who need to be held accountable. We can trust and hope that in every situation, love will conquer all fear.

These decisions we make all tie into a universal point, that we are more than conquerors through Jesus. We choose love for others because Jesus loves us. We have hope in the midst of a storm, because Jesus has already won the battle. We protect those that need it because Jesus has protected our hearts from death.

We are more than able to choose love; Jesus has loved you and I from the start. Seeking the best in people and putting them first is truly loving. We love others because we know that in the end, Jesus wants us to unify as one. We are stronger together and can be unshakable if we invest in each other. This world can drag you down a hole in a hurry, but having a faithful brother there for you will defeat all division and hate.

"And above all these put on love, which binds everything together in perfect harmony." Colossians 3:14

Chapter 6:
Finding Your Purpose

"Your potential is the sum of all the possibilities God has for your life." - **Charles Stanley**

Everyone has a purpose in life. You are called by the Most High to do something so special and ordinary. It will take some time and trust to figure it out, but all will work for His glory. Your life holds so much value.

A lot of times, we catch ourselves wanting to dictate our lives and futures. We make sure everything lines up perfectly to achieve what *we* want, and if we don't- we're failures. Our lives are over. Something I have grown to realize over the years is that I serve a Big God. One big enough to rule the universe, and He knows my name! He promises me He has a plan for me, so I trust Him. I know that however things work out, He will be glorified.

During the summer of 2019, I was scheduled for some "big" events. In August I would be attending the Areacode Underclass games at the MLB Youth Academy in Compton, California. I was pumped. This was a really big event, and I was super excited.

I hopped on a plane along with my mom and David (sorry dad, duty calls!) and we made our way out to California. That night we received all of our cool gear and merchandise, all being labeled for the Yankees (don't worry, I'll always rep the Nationals).

Boy was I ready to get on the field. This was a highly scouted event from Major League teams, and I would be playing against some of the top talent in the country. Game on.

The first day came and I was riding the hype train. I was overwhelmed, impressed, and nervous about how I would look. I wanted to showcase myself and make my name known.

All about me.

We went through warmups and pre-game batting practice and finally got to the game. I was taking it all in while still getting ready to play. It was show time.

All about me.

Long story short, that game ended with me going 0-1 at the plate and 2 errors behind the dish catching. Great start to a week where I would show how much I have to offer. I was down after the game, mad at what I could have done better, and was eager for the next day. I wanted to really show them I was worth it.

All about me.

The next day was a double header, where we would play one in the afternoon and one under the lights that night. I showed up and was told I wouldn't be playing the first game, being there were 2 other catchers on the team, but I would catch the night game. Bummer.

I stood on the line during the National Anthem, shades on, and just looked around. There were so many faces there and so many different personalities. I wondered if they knew Christ.

And then it hit me! This is my opportunity to showcase Jesus, not me! I was brought across the country to play for Jesus written on my jersey. This wasn't about me.

During the first game I surveyed the dugout looking who I could start a conversation with. I talked to so many people and they all had such different backgrounds. Some of them spoke of Christ.

Finally the night game came, and I was scheduled to be the starting catcher. I had gone through warmups with my pitcher, making sure he was ready, and kept a smile on my face. Boy was that guy nervous!

The game started and it was a good one. We faced a pitcher who was throwing really hard, and shut us down the first inning. It was time for us to take the field.

Here we go.

After a clean first inning, the game moved along and our team did great. While I went 2-3 that game, I also caught 4 clean innings with numerous blocks and throwing completions. My trip had turned around.

The next day was beautiful and we had the morning game. I arrived and they told me I would be leading off. While I was thrilled, I knew there was a greater spot for me here to promote Jesus.

We went through warmups and then headed over to the field. I spoke to some of the guys who were walking with me, and they all had open hearts and were loving individuals.

The other team took the field and I moved into the on deck circle. I timed up the pitcher, took a few deep breaths and was ready. Game on.

I walked up and greeted both the catcher and the umpire, wishing them the best and giving them a tap on their shoulders. I stepped in, ready to face the pitcher. Here goes nothing.

The first pitch I see whizzes past me- ball. I step out for a minute, deep breath, step back in, and get ready for the next pitch. He threw it and I was all in on it. I swung. CRACK!

To my amazement, as I rounded first I saw the outfielder look up and stop moving. I hit a home run.

I rounded the bases and came to home plate with a big smile. After a little point to the sky, I got back into the dugout and got a bunch of high fives from my teammates. I was glad I could help the team, but I was even more happy about what happened after I touched home. With everyone watching at the beginning of the game, hundreds of people saw me thank God. He gave me a platform to use.

While the start of the trip was not ideal in *my* eyes, the overall experience didn't go too bad after all. After we got home from the event, I got in contact with the pitcher that I hit the home run off of. He is now in one of the Bible verse group chats. Crazy! When we remind ourselves to work for God and

His glory, and set that as our number one priority, all else will fall into place. One of my favorite verses about that is Proverbs 3:5-6, which reads, "Trust in the Lord with all your heart and lean not on your own understanding; in all ways acknowledge Him and He will make your path straight."

What would our lives look like if we walk the path God has created for us? If you truly want to glorify Him, trust with all of your heart that He will make a way. And even if the final result isn't what you intended for it to be, your path will remain straight and full of prosperity. God promises that.

Besides, we serve the God of the universe.

Our True Calling

I've had a lot of conversations with people who wonder about their future. Things like what kind of job they will have, what they want to be when they grow up, or how many accomplishments they want to achieve. The conversation is so centered around me, me, me and looks no farther beyond what we want for ourselves.

Everytime this happens, I respond with the same thing. "Our purpose in life is to promote Christ."

Now you may be thinking, "For sure! I do that already. I trust God." But at the same time, you are bouncing unexpectedly from job to job, you are anxious about winning some award, and you want to be a Hall of Fame athlete. While all of these are fine, reality is that's not for God- that's for you. You want to be the center of attention. You want to be the best. You want to be well-known.

Goals are good and I love them, but they can't consume us. When we do things only to accomplish them for our personal benefit, we make it all about ourselves. The truth is, it's not about us and never will be. It's about Jesus and what He does and has already done. Our purpose will be brought to light when we bring Him to life. Acknowledge Him, and He will make your path straight.

"And whatever you do in word or deed, do all in the name of the Lord Jesus, giving thanks to God the Father through Him." Colossians 3:17

The Greatest Gift

During the process of writing this book, my grandfather was finishing up writing one as well. Papa, what David and I call him, was very interested and spent a lot of his time digging into Scripture. He mailed a copy of his new book to me so I could read over it and when I opened the first page, I saw something that stuck out to me.

"The greatest present that one man can give to another is an introduction to God's gift, salvation through Jesus Christ."

Boom. Plain and simple. Papa got straight to the point and made it as clear as it could be. We are called to be disciples.

When we talk about purpose, this right here explains it all. The usual conversation about purpose consists of accomplishments, goals, and feats. We begin to worry about our future careers, future accolades, and future success, if any.

"Purpose" has been transformed from the *why* we do things, to now focusing on *what* we do.

Like Papa said, salvation is the greatest thing we can give to others. Bringing light to a room of darkness is most important. Spreading faith and hope while showing love far surpasses any award we win. In this case, we are no longer living for ourselves, but living for Christ.

I'm sure you are wondering to yourself, "What really is *my* purpose though? What path will my life go down?" The answer to those questions comes in your faith. Believe that God will make a way, because He promises He will. And in the meantime, put others before yourself. Show love. Spread hope. In the midst of your efforts in promoting Christ, He will open up a door that is perfect for you. He promises that.

Faith in this situation says that even though I cannot see my future, I know who holds it. Even though I have no idea what to do with my life right now, I am going to serve others. Even though life has taken a turn for the worse, I will continue to spread hope and believe that there is a greater God who loves and calls me His own.

If you have already found a field where you are comfortable and feel like you need to be in, that is great! The key now is to take advantage of each opportunity you get in that field. God opened the door for you already, and that doesn't mean you stop bringing hope like you were before. Continue to persevere in faith and show gratitude, while spreading love and positivity.

So when it's all said and done, remember our true purpose here on earth. We are here to help those around us. We are here to influence our peers in the most positive way. We are here to promote Christ and His love. We are called to be disciples of the Gospel.

And when things don't seem to go our way, don't get down. Don't quit. There's a God inside of you who is much more powerful. Because of Him, you are more than a conqueror.

"Ye are of God, little children, and have overcome them: because greater is he that is in you, than he that is in the world." 1 John 4:4

Chapter 7:
Work for the Good

"Relying on God has to start all over everyday, as if nothing has yet been done." **–C. S. Lewis**

How you do anything is how you do everything.
Throughout our lives we will be challenged; whether it be school, an audition, a tough workout, a business presentation, you name it. If we pick and choose which tasks we give our all and which tasks we slack off, it creates imbalance. While you may be excelling in one field, you are failing in another. This mindset will only get you so far.

I've had numerous friends that were absolute studs at their sport, but didn't excel in the classroom. I've seen many students that were really smart but their attitudes made people not want to help them. Instead of being the best at one thing, strive to excel in all fields and aspects in your life.

I've never been a big fan of the phrase "being the best." Many feel differently, so here is my standpoint.

First, let me get things straight. Of course I want to try to be my best and perform to the highest capability I can in whatever I do. It would be foolish to attempt something you don't give your all on. However, you cannot let this mindset dictate what you chase after, and how you treat people. When we say we want to be the best at something, we want to succeed in that particular field. It could be making it to the Major Leagues, it could be growing up to be a lawyer, or it could even be the best student in your class. But, telling ourselves to be the best is only making it about *you*. While you're so convinced you need to succeed and perform at your highest ability, you lose sight of a chance to impact others around you, and ultimately what God has in store. If we limit ourselves to chasing after one goal, we could be turning away from where God really needs you to go! Chasing our own dreams is what our heart desires, not God.

Again, don't get me wrong. In your mind, you can strive to be the greatest ever. Tell yourself to dominate this workout. Tell yourself to work harder than ever. Tell yourself nobody is studying more than you. But the key is to not tell everyone else around you. Nothing benefits from bragging to others what we're doing or how hard we're working. This is making things all about us, and besides, who are you trying to prove? You are loved by the King of Kings.

All in all, the lesson here is to find a way to motivate yourself without letting others dictate how you work. Go 110% in everything you do. But remember, God has a plan for you to prosper. Let Him take the reins, and follow His steps.

It'll take a leap of faith, but you'll be pleasantly surprised at what He has for your future (Romans 8:18).

My Support System

When I tell you that my dad, my brother, and I are constantly moving- we are constantly moving. I'm talking about four to five hours a day of either working out, playing some game, or bettering our baseball skills. The three of us look out and support each other every single day.

A typical day looks like this. David and I usually start the morning off on a turf field. We throw, run, and maybe even toss around a football. Following lunch we head to a baseball field to hit with my dad, who hobbles around the outfield shagging balls. Lastly Dave and I conclude our night with a lift down in the basement.

I tell you these things not to brag or boast about how much we workout; someone else's opinion of me and my hobbies means nothing. I say this to emphasize the point of working for a good purpose. We don't spend five hours a day working to become the greatest Major League Baseball player ever. We spend five hours a day working together because we love each other, and want to promote Christ while doing so. Our work now may bring us to someone in need of the Gospel. If all we care about is hitting home runs, we may miss out on that opportunity.

My dad is one of the most loving and caring men you will ever see. He truly has a genuine heart who puts others first. While he may be tired, or hurting after a long day, he still will throw balls to Dave and I at 8 o'clock at night. If he just finished an afternoon job, he will be the first one to offer us a workout spot where we can meet. Dad is supportive, kind hearted, and puts his family first. I'm so glad I have parents like my mom and my dad.

David is the same way. While he continues to grow and mature, he has quickly learned that his impact on others is most important. The countless hours we spend with each other have only made us closer and stronger together. And again, we don't seek to be the greatest of all time. We seek to bring hope and spread love everywhere we go, using our work as a platform and way to reach new places. Besides, we know we are already the greatest in God's eyes.

Having a support group is huge. There are a lot of people out there who maybe don't have the most supportive families or friends, and I understand that. That is tough. But God presents His strongest battles to His strongest warriors. That friend who keeps putting you down, maybe you are being called to bring him up. Your dad who keeps bashing you about a mistake you made in your game the other day, maybe you tell him that you appreciate him and love him, no matter what he does or doesn't achieve. And in the end, you will *always* have the strongest supporter of all in Jesus Christ. Coming from the Son of God who died in your place because He loves you, take His word for it. He has never forsaken you.

Just Do It!

Frequently on social media, people post their workouts and rave about how hard they work. I always wonder why they feel the need to tell others. Then it hit me- insecurity.

When we start to hype ourselves, it shows our need for someone's affirmation. Telling a friend "you work harder than him" does nothing but put the spotlight on yourself. Don't feel the need for the spotlight. Simply grind without searching for pats on your back. Nobody cares about how hard you are working, they care only about results. Instead of checking how many people are liking your last post, get some work done.

Hard work is often talked about, but what exactly is hard work? The only way to excel at something (unless you have a God given talent) is to put the time in. If you're looking to get in better shape, it's going to take time! Rome wasn't built in a day; your body is not going to change after a week. If you are trying to raise that C to an A, you need to study! Thirty minutes reviewing your notes isn't going to cut it. If you are putting together a quality presentation, it will take extended research and numerous days to complete.

There will be days we don't feel like doing anything. Our bodies might hurt, or we are mentally worn out. Something that helps me is to simply say "just do it." If you really think about it, every task we complete in life, we need to just do it. We are more than capable of studying, running a mile, or writing a brilliant paper. We have to just do it. Yes we may have pain but that pain is temporary. Yes we may be lost but we can always learn. When you tell yourself to simply do a task, your mind will be at ease and you will have the confidence to "just do it!"

Preparation

Failing to plan is planning to fail. If you don't structure your days and lose track of what needs to get done, little will get accomplished. Wake up with a sense of urgency, know what you want to complete that day and get to it. Procrastinating will only lead to forgetting about it.

Putting off work is another struggle we all deal with. Oftentimes when we have all day to do something, we wait until the last minute. We spend the majority of the day watching shows, eating junk, or laying around and then before we know it, it's 8 pm. Now you're tired and don't feel like working. Guess it will have to get done tomorrow.

Instead of looking at work as a punishment, look at it as a gift. If God has given you a healthy mind and body, you shouldn't complain about work. There are plenty of people who would jump at the opportunity to work but can't for one reason or another, or go to college but can't afford it. There are military veterans who have sustained life-changing injuries who would love to have their health back in order to live the life they once had. If we are fortunate enough for God to have given us healthy minds and bodies, we should use them to their fullest extent.

Today Is The Day!

Think about your normal routine each day. Let's imagine it is a Monday morning and you are getting ready to leave for work. You wake up super tired after getting minimal sleep last night. You wait until the last minute to get out of bed, rush to get dressed then head downstairs. You take a look at the time and you are already running late, so you skip breakfast. Once you arrive at work you receive a mountain of paperwork you have to complete. The day slowly goes by and you start to get annoyed. It's been a long day, you are tired and hungry, and you have a bunch of work to do. Bummer.

If this sounds like you, don't feel like you're alone! We all have days where we don't feel like doing *anything.* And because we choose not to do anything, we stay the same. We don't spend time growing in our faith, we don't complete that assignment we really wanted to do, or maybe we didn't get a chance to do that home workout we found online. If you look at the whole scheme of things, we have not spent that day to its fullest intent.

Another one of my favorite verses comes from Psalm 188:24, which reads:

"This is the day the Lord has made,
We will rejoice and be glad in it."

Now you may be thinking to yourself, "I've heard this verse millions of times sung at church!" But this verse is actually the beginning of understanding purpose. The way we approach each and every day will determine how much or how little we will complete over the course of our lives.

Imagine if everyday when we woke up, we told ourselves that *today* is the day I grow with Christ. Today is the day where I accomplish what I could not yesterday. Today is the day that I will put others first. Today is the day where I thank God for waking me up!

When we do not take advantage of each day, we slowly become more and more selfish about our time. Reality is, Jesus Christ is coming soon- and it could be tomorrow. Who knows? But the fact of the matter is that we are not promised another day. We are not promised second chances. We are not promised do overs.

We are promised one thing- grace. God has forever loved you and me and because of that, we have the chance to live on forever. Our time is essential. Each day we have a choice to speak life or drain it. Each day we have a choice to put others before ourselves. But if we choose to approach the day like just another day, the significance is lost in our hearts.

You are not too late. You are not too far gone! You are not too old or too young. But you are able. Able to choose to take advantage of this day to help yourself, and ultimately to help others.

Life is precious. We have the chance to bring love to people who need it the most, so let's take advantage of that. Imagine if we woke up everyday with the mindset of today is the day I make a change.

Today is the day I help a brother in need.

Today is the day I put others before myself.

Today is the day I forgive what is hurting me.

Today is the day I combat fear with love.

Today is the day that God has given me, so I will rejoice and be glad.

It's Not Always About Winning

Sports are very similar to life. There will be ups and downs, but through it all you must trust the process and stay loyal to the people around you. Most people play sports for the thrill of the game, but everyone wants to win. If you are not trying to win and do your best, you may want to consider another hobby.

However winning is something that should not define us. If we play only to win, we are actually playing with the fear of losing. The loss is what we can not handle. Even if we win, what does that gain us? People that play to win every game will never be satisfied with just one win. Every time they play they have to come out on top, which leads to overwhelming disappointment when they lose. There is never enough satisfaction. This is very similar to people who gamble; there is never enough winning. Gamblers seek to surpass their previous winnings and because of that, do not quit until they do so. This often leads to losing even more money.

Instead of playing to win the game, we should play to win for the love of the game. While playing to win is playing in fear, playing for God and for the people around you is playing out of love. If all we care about is the dub, even if we do win, fear will control our lives. Until the next game is determined, the fear of losing will continue to be in the back of your mind. But when you play with love for Christ and others, you realize that the win does not matter. What matters is your impact on those people on that particular day. A win is just a bonus.

If you look at the society we live in now, there is little contentment in people. Things always have to be bigger, better... faster. There is always the fear that it is not good enough. Truth be told- we are already good enough in God's eyes. He loves us the way we are, even if we think we are nothing. Jesus died for you and me, knowing that we are lost sinners. His love has already conquered our defeats.

Now you may be thinking to yourself, "What is this guy talking about? Why would I ever play a game not to win?" Of course we all want to win, but the truth is we get more out of our play when we play out of love. When we play to win, we feel like we are of less value if we lose. But if we play out of love, we are reminded that winning does not define who God says we are. In turn this will help us to live selflessly and to put others before ourselves.

I truly believe that in a competition between two teams of similar skill, whichever team leads with love will win the game. I'm not saying if you pray to God before the game He will bless you with a win, because God doesn't care who wins. I am saying that if the team plays for Jesus and each other, love will conquer over all. Our wins are another opportunity to give the glory to God. While He may not determine who wins, He is the one who gives us the ability to play. So when something good happens, or even when something bad happens, always choose gratitude.

Playing to win can also lead to being prideful. If we get too focused on our wins and accomplishments, all of our attention turns to us. We will no longer look out for others. But if we acknowledge our wins as a gift, winning becomes less important. We won't be as focused on our individual achievements. Instead we will see a win as just another opportunity to thank God, play in His glory, and show others our true thankfulness.

Winning on the Biggest Stage

In the fall of 2019, the Washington Nationals took home a World Series championship after an unbelievable run throughout the whole year. They battled hard through the postseason and worked for the team more than working for themselves. Most importantly, many of them were working for Christ.

I can remember so many things about their spectacular title run. My brother and I were in attendance for an electric Wild Card game and also were fortunate enough to attend the first ever World Series game in the nation's capital. I watched most of the first round of the playoffs from a hotel room in Florida. I also remember I couldn't even watch Game 7 of the World Series because I was on an overnight school retreat. But, there is one thing I remember in particular that has stuck with me to this day.

A few days before the World Series started, an article came out about the Nationals' third baseman, Anthony Rendon. Now if you don't know who that is, this guy is a perennial stud. Not only does he hit homers and make crazy plays, but he shows love to everyone he meets. I clicked on the article which was titled, "I want to be more Christian than ballplayer."

Immediately after I read that a huge smile appeared on my face. Hearing that from someone like Rendon was amazing and shows how much good we really can bring to people's hearts. This guy truly gets it. I continued down the article and found this quote- "If I just try to stay in the Word and try to surround myself with good people and have a good community, I think that will just guide me on that path."

Anthony Rendon is someone who hits 30 bombs a year. He makes Gold Glove plays at third base. He leads the league in average. This guy is at the top of his game, and while he could have very easily promoted himself, he promoted Christ.

Besides the Nationals winning that series, Rendon had himself a solid performance smacking 2 home runs over seven games. But he could care less. He realizes that win or loss, strikeout or homerun, his life is a gift. Being able to play is a gift. Having the opportunity to play a game in front of tens of thousands of people for a world championship is a gift.

Perspective.

The last thing that stuck with me was his comments about his future. "You definitely think about it. You want to plan for the future," he told the paper. "But I've come to learn your plans don't always come to fruition. Obviously, with my faith, too, I don't want to seem like it's all about me, me, me. It takes away from what I do for Him, for the Lord."

The moment we think we control the outcome of our life is the moment we deny God from working in it. It's not about us. It's about what He has done, what He is doing and what He promises to do.

No matter the outcome, we are already winners through Christ. We are already more than conquerors. Our platforms are so important for us to take advantage of. Not for ourselves, but to promote Jesus. When the world is watching and looking for an answer of hope, the story of the Gospel will never fail.

Chapter 8: Meaningless

"He who lays up treasures on earth spends his life backing away from his treasures. To him, death is loss. He who lays up treasures in heaven looks forward to eternity; he's moving daily toward his treasures. To him, death is gain."
- Randy Alcorn

In the Bible, there is a story of a man named Job. This man, along with his big family, was very wealthy and owned a bunch of land. You could say that Job had all he would ever need in life.

But the only thing he needed for happiness was his faith. Job was very faithful to God and truly trusted Him. He followed Christ and fled evil. He was an upstanding individual in the community. Besides all of his wealth, Job impacted the people around him through his actions. He truly cared for others and chose love countlessly.

One day Satan appeared in front of God and claimed that Job was only faithful to Him because He had blessed Job abundantly. Satan challenged God, and said that if He would allow punishment onto Job, that Job would lose faith. God accepted the challenge and knew Job would be in for a tough road ahead. All in one day, Job found out that his livestock, servants, and all ten children died. His skin then began to sore and rot. However, Job remained faithful and continued to stay in prayer.

Job's friends came to his house to see him. They asked questions like, "What did you do to God to make Him this mad at you?" Job began to wonder the same thing himself. He started questioning God and demanded an answer. God then spoke to Job.

As Job began to ask why all of this torment was being brought upon him, God showed him pictures of the universe. He explained how diverse and perfect it is when it all works together. Job realized that he could not comprehend God's wisdom and gave up his anger. He humbled himself and thanked God for His guidance.

But that was not all. Soon Job was replenished with all of his needs, except this time it was doubled. Job was given back all of his belongings he had and became healthy again. He used this story to convey God's wisdom to other people.

Why am I telling this story? Good question. There are a lot of things we can take away here.

First let's get things straight. God did not replenish Job because he "passed the test." That was not the reasoning behind the gift. But He did deliver a better alternative than where Job was before, which is true in all of our lives. God promises to lead us through the storm no matter how rough it gets, if we trust Him.

Job realized something we all can learn from. God is too knowledgeable for us to comprehend. He moves all of the pieces just right to fit the puzzle. When we think something may be wrong, the truth is He knows exactly why it is right. In the midst of a storm, yes Job felt some doubt. It is completely fine and ordinary to feel doubt and be anxious. But we cannot let that define us. The moment we begin to let stress and fear take over our minds, we immediately close off God's guidance and wisdom He has for us.

Lastly, Job gives us an unusual outlook on life. When everything was taken away from him, Job never cared about losing it. He immediately went to God and asked what he could do better to glorify Him. What he did not do was start questioning why he lost his favorite sheep! Job realized that this life and what it holds means nothing. What we accomplish, gain, or inherit on earth has no significance in our place in heaven.

This world is meaningless.

I'm not saying what you do here on earth doesn't matter, because as the previous chapters describe it most definitely does. What I am saying is that everything within the world, everything we can earn, everything we can accomplish, is meaningless. So many times we are too concerned with:

Clothing
Shoes
Social Media Followers
Cars
Houses

Money

Fame

Power

Popularity

Winning

Sports

The list could go on! There are so many things we can attain in life that in the real scope of things, they mean nothing. You don't get a better seat in heaven for having the most possessions. You do not get to have a secret handshake with God because you have the most followers. You definitely aren't worth more than someone else because you have more money.

Reality is we have all fallen short and are sinners. We have no right to put ourselves above someone else. So when it comes to material goods, the less we care about them the better. The less we show off our belongings the better. Because what is it really doing? We are trying to let others know we are worth more. Posting pictures of all of our worth and materials is only searching for affirmations and "likes."

I'm not saying if you are blessed with the opportunity to have money or fame, to completely ignore it. When we are given things like these, the key is to remember how to use them. Instead of buying things just to buy, give back to communities that need it. When given a platform to speak, instead of gloating about yourself, praise God! He is the one who holds it all, not us. When opportunities arise, the best thing to do is give Him the glory.

As the chapter continues we will dive more into this discussion, but for now let's remember our real significance on earth. We aren't here to have as many cars we can in our garage. We are not called to boast about how many Super Bowl rings we have won. Our true purpose in life is to impact those around us and shine light on them through our actions. Our life is not about us. The moment we choose to live selflessly, our lives will then be turned on putting others before ourselves, just like Jesus did.

Understanding the Moment

Several years ago I attended Sunday School and to this day I remember this particular sermon. I walked in the gym with some of my friends and we sat down on the bottom bleacher, awaiting our counselor for the day. He walked in with a long piece of string and I remember wondering to myself, "Why in the world is he dragging around string?"

As he began to speak, I noticed a small part at the end of the string was colored in black marker. At the time I didn't understand why he would color such a small amount of the string, but once he explained it I was all ears.

He told all of us to look at this long string, probably around 10 feet, and focus on this black colored area. I remember he said, "See this small colored piece? This is our time on earth. The rest of this string and forever on after that is our eternity in Heaven."

I was in awe. I imagined a never ending piece of string that covered so much more area than the small, colored piece at the beginning.

I then began to think about the black colored piece. How could I think that this small amount of time is even worth comparing to *eternity?* We get so consumed sometimes about our present state that we lose focus on true peace, being eternal life after death.

I realized that day that my priorities can not be of this temporary world. I can not live for glorification in this short life. The focus must be on the Father, and His Holy Place, since He is who gives us this life anyway.

When we invest ourselves in the world and what it holds, we fear death. We worry about losing all of our materials, leaving behind valuables, and dismissing our own fame and power. Our motives are so consumed in this short life that we disregard our interest for the eternal one.

However, if we invest ourselves in Christ and His promises, death is a gain. We no longer fear losing things we have accomplished or obtained here on earth. We look forward to eternity and the treasures that will soon be revealed. Our eyes are now on the Father.

Again, I'm not saying this life is not important. As we have discussed throughout this book, we are called to be disciples of Christ. Our lives are meant to thrive for the good. But we cannot get consumed by the world in the process. This world holds many things, most of them temporary, and if we invest too much in them we will lose sight of what God is trying to show us. Our eyes will then be on the world.

If you buy into this concept, I truly think it will change your life altogether. Everything works together in our relationship with Jesus. If we flee temptation and disregard consumption of the world, we have faith that God will provide. We remain hopeful that our future is much brighter than our present. And if we truly believe that God is sovereign and greater than any trial we may face, we love and put all of our trust in Him. We are now more than conquerors.

What does it benefit us to gain the whole world? Our lives are temporary, but our souls are eternal. Keeping this mindset will allow us to dismiss this world and it's temptations. We now can be anxious for nothing because Heaven is eternal. We now can let go of the illusion of control, because Heaven is eternal. We now can let God take our battles, because Heaven is eternal.

A phrase I like to say is "Keep your eyes up." When our eyes are down we cannot see what lies ahead. We are trapped in the moment. But when our eyes are up, our focus is on our promised future of eternal life.

"I will lift up my eyes to the hills- from whence comes my help? My help comes from the Lord, who made heaven and earth." Psalms 121:1-2

"Love not the world, neither the things that are in the world. If any man love the world, the love of the Father is not in him." 1 John 2:15

"For what shall it profit a man, if he shall gain the whole world, and lose his own soul?" Mark 8:36

Chapter 9:
An Act of Love

"Christ literally walked in our shoes." **- Tim Keller**

Throughout this book we talked about showing love and treating others like Jesus. As Christians this is what we are called to do- spread hope and bring joy. But the truth is, being nice to people is not the way to eternal life.

In the Bible, God describes a place of peace and love that is full of angels, Jesus, and Himself. This place is called Heaven, and it is a forever state of life.

Now before God made man, the Big Three stood alone in Heaven (Father, Son, Holy Spirit). And the truth is, they were at peace. God did not lack anything because He was already perfect.

Then, God created man. Man was intended to live forever with God in perfect peace, until sin entered the world. Because of man's first sin in the Garden of Eden, we are now forever separated from God.

But God truly does not want that. God loves you. He loves me, too. He loves everyone on earth to its fullest. So what did He do?

He sent Jesus. The perfect man who knew no sin. Jesus lived a sinless life and was brought to earth for one thing:

"For God so loved the world that He gave His only begotten Son, that whoever believes in Him should not perish but have everlasting life." John 3:16

Jesus came to save the world from sin. God loves us so much that He sent the only Son He had to die in our place. That, my friend, is love.

Jesus was beaten, mocked, and finally crucified on the cross for no wrongdoings. He was not a criminal, not a sinner, not a crook. He died for you and me so that if we call on Him, we can live forever in eternity.

Our salvation is not given by works; we cannot earn it. Jesus' grace is given to us as a *gift*. He wants a relationship with us and seeks to lead your life with love. We just have to let Him.

If you have never accepted Jesus in your heart, today might be the day. As we discussed earlier in this book, today is the day to change your life. Today is the day we let Christ lead and we follow. Today is the day your sin is cleansed.

If you truly believe that Jesus died for your sin and rose from the dead, you will be saved. The Bible says that. It takes a step forward, leaving your old creature behind, and opening your heart to a new beginning with Jesus.

If you want to fully commit to Christ, all it takes is a simple prayer. It may go like this:

God, thank you for your never ending love.

Thank you for forgiving me of my sin, time after time. I know I am wrong and have turned against You.

I realize I cannot conquer this life without You. I ask you to come into my heart and be my personal Lord and Savior. I trust that Your plan is greater than mine.

Help me glorify You through my actions and words, and work in my heart for the goodness of others. My life is Yours to hold.

Amen.

I'm so thankful for God's love, and so thankful you can recognize it with me! His grace is a gift. Take it. He will change your life if we open our hearts and let Him.

If you just accepted Jesus, congratulations! Welcome to the family of God. As my brother or sister, I hope and pray this decision further impacts your decisions and your life. We all have a chance to make a difference. With Jesus at the forefront, there is nothing we can't do.

Now that you have made this choice, let's start this journey down Christ's path. Remember He knows far more than we do, and can lead us to greater things than we can ever imagine. Because of His grace, we are more than conquerors.

Chapter 10:
Final Thoughts

"True faith means holding nothing back. It means putting every hope in God's fidelity to His Promises." **-Francis Chan**

If you have stuck with me this far, thank you! This is the end of my first book. I hope and pray that these words have helped and inspired you to believe in yourself, trust Christ, and grow to be an upstanding and loving individual.

I can honestly say that writing this book was not easy. At times I would struggle with finding words to write or worry about the content that is included. But as we have discussed, there is no reason to worry. God already loves us for who we are.

I hope that after reading you take a step back and really analyze your current situation. Open your heart to guidance and understanding. God is always tugging on our sleeve, it's just a matter of if we listen or not.

I pray that you start to live with an open heart and step out of your comfort zone. Only when we seek change is where we will see a difference. Staying the same leads to contentment, and that's not what defines our lives. We were made to thrive.

I hope that you begin to find peace within yourself, and remember that greater is He than anything or anyone in this world. Jesus has already conquered the grave. You are already forgiven. When life throws you a curveball, remember you *will not* strike out. The Creator of the universe calls you His child!

I pray that your faith grows stronger than ever. When you give Him your all, I promise you will see Him more clearly. Our own understanding will only bring us so far, but with Christ we are capable of moving mountains.

I hope that you grow to persevere, forgive, and practice each virtue of love. Don't let fear control your life. You are so much stronger! Put others first and in turn, you will see them love in return. If Jesus forgives us daily from our sin, we can forgive our brother in his fault as well.

I pray that you trust in God and His promises for your life. Your life has a purpose. You are here for a reason. Trust that He will provide! And while doing so, spread hope and love to those around you. The only "career" we should strive to work in is being a disciple of Jesus.

I hope that your work may come to fruition, but also remember to work for the good. Seeking personal benefit and praise will trap you in the lie of temporary fame. But when Jesus is at the center of our actions, our work conveys gratitude and faith in His love.

I pray that you leave behind the temporary wants and achievements, and seek first the Kingdom. God promises eternity to those who love Him. We benefit nothing from gaining the world, because it is so temporary. But if we seek the Father and eternal love, that on the other hand will last forever.

And finally, I hope that if you originally did not know Christ, you met Him today! He loves you more than you can think. Accepting Him in your heart is the first step to living out His promises and using His guidance for our lives.

Seek Jesus first. He has never left you and never will. He loves you! I love you. Take on this challenge of life. If it were easy, everyone would be happy. But this world contains storms. How will you bounce back? How will you be strong?

Jesus. Trust Him. Satan has no shot at competing with a heart led by Christ. Put Him first, and all else will fall into place.

Besides, we are already more than conquerors through Christ.

Favorite Verses Section

"For I am convinced that neither death nor life, neither angels nor demons, neither the present nor the future, nor any powers, neither height nor depth, nor anything else in all creation, will be able to separate us from the love of God that is in Christ Jesus our Lord." Romans 8:38-39

"Ye are of God, little children, and have overcome them: because greater is he that is in you, than he that is in the world." 1 John 4:4

"Greater love has no one than this: to lay down one's life for one's friends." John 15:13

"Be strong and courageous. Do not be afraid or terrified because of them, or the LORD your God goes with you; he will never leave you nor forsake you." Deuteronomy 31:6

"The Lord is my light and my salvation; whom shall I fear? The Lord is the stronghold of my life; of whom shall I be afraid?" Psalm 27:12

"There is no fear in love. But perfect love drives out fear, because fear has to do with punishment. The one who fears is not made perfect in love." John 4:18

"What, then, shall we say in response to these things? If God is for us, who can be against us?" Romans 8:31

"Jesus looked at them and said, 'With man it is impossible, but not with God. For all things are possible with God.'" Mark 10:27

"Casting all your anxieties on him, because he cares for you." 1 Peter 5:7

"I can do all things through him who strengthens me." Philippians 4:13

"Trust in the LORD with all your heart, and do not lean on your own understanding. In all your ways acknowledge him, and he will make straight your paths." Proverbs 3:5-6

"And we know that in all things God works for the good of those who love him, who have been called according to his purpose." Romans 8:28

"For I reckon that the sufferings of this present time are not worthy to be compared with the glory which shall be revealed in us." Romans 8:18

"For what shall it profit a man, if he shall gain the whole world, and lose his own soul?" Mark 8:36

"Thy word have I hid in mine heart, that I might not sin against thee." Psalm 119:11

"For God so loved the world, that he gave his only begotten Son, that whosoever believeth in him should not perish, but have everlasting life." John 3:16

"Do not be afraid, for I am with you." Genesis 26:24

"Do not fret- it only causes harm." Psalm 37:8

"Rejoice in the Lord always. I will say it again: Rejoice! Let your gentleness be evident to all. The Lord is near. Do not be anxious about anything, but in every situation, by prayer and petition, with thanksgiving, present your requests to God. And the peace of God, which transcends all understanding, will guard your hearts and your minds in Christ Jesus. Finally, brothers and sisters, whatever is true, whatever is noble, whatever is right, whatever is pure, whatever is lovely, whatever is admirable—if anything is excellent or praiseworthy—think about such things. Whatever you have learned or received or heard from me, or seen in me—put it into practice. And the God of peace will be with you." Philippians 4:4-9

"The Lord is my shepherd; I shall not want. He maketh me to lie down in green pastures: he leadeth me beside the still waters. He restoreth my soul: he leadeth me in the paths of righteousness for his name's sake. Yea, though I walk through the valley of the shadow of death, I will fear no evil: for thou art with me; thy rod and thy staff they comfort me. Thou preparest a table before me in the presence of mine enemies: thou anointest my head with oil; my cup runneth over. Surely goodness and mercy shall follow me all the days of my life: and I will dwell in the house of the Lord for ever." Psalm 23

"Jesus Christ the same yesterday, today, and forever." Hebrews 13:8

"Keep your heart with all vigilance, for from it flow the springs of life." Proverbs 4:23

"Set your mind on things above, not on earth." Colossians 3:2

"Him, being delivered by the determinate counsel and foreknowledge of God, ye have taken, and by wicked hands have crucified and slain: Whom God hath raised up, having loosed the pains of death: because it was not possible that he should be holden of it." Acts 2:23-24

"Nay, in all these things we are more than conquerors through him that loved us." Romans 8:37

Acknowledgements

Mom- Thank you for all of your never ending support and countless efforts to make me a better human. Everyday you center your time around David and I, and make us your first priority. You are a strong woman and a great mom. I love you!

Dad- Thank you for being the best dad I could ask for. All of the long days and nights never went unnoticed. All of your words of wisdom will also never be forgotten. Thank you for your selfless heart. I love you.

David- I'm so grateful to be able to say I have a brother like you. You push me harder everyday to excel in all aspects of life. I hope you know how special you are to me. I love you man.

Grandma and Papa- You guys are the definition of amazing grandparents. The support and love you give to me is unmatched. I'm so happy I have both of you in my life. I love you guys!

Yeye- The definition of positivity. I love you Yeye. Thank you for consistently bringing happiness, kindness, and love.

Coach Spinks and the Thomas Pullen coaching staff- Some of the "realest" coaches I've ever met. Thank you for leading me through middle school and helping me learn more about myself. Love!

Coach Ryan, Coach T and the Riverdale coaching staff- To the coaches who grew my passion for Christ, I thank you guys from the bottom of my heart. You all are true role models and love everyone you see. Thank you for your support, guidance, and confidence in me.

Coach Sos, Coach Andy, Coach Raph, Coach Martinez, Coach McNair, and the whole McNamara coaching staff- Thank you for not only being great coaches, but great mentors and friends. You all have taught me so much and believed in me from the start. All of the support, help, and love will never go unseen. Thank you for also practicing serious patience with me!

Mr. Glover Hines- Thank you for being such a mentor and class act. I appreciate you allowing me to learn from you and grow in my knowledge in Christ. Love coach!

Coach Jackson and the Liberty Baseball coaching staff- Thank you for believing in me coach! A true leader that serves his community. Looking forward to being around you more in years to come.

Ben Blackwell- To someone who has challenged me to take leaps in my faith, thank you for leading me in the right directions bro. You've impacted my life so positively and continue to lead others to Christ. Love brother!

Brando- You are an inspiration my man! Continue to smile and be yourself. I love ya!

Ms. Homayouni- Thank you for your trust in me and allowing me to highlight Noah and his love for others. I know his life truly made a difference for those around him and he is continually watching over you and your family.

To the rest of my family, all of my friends, teammates, teachers, Toddy, Mr. Aaron Everhart, Mr. Steve Barrick, Coach Davis, Coach Ellis, Coach Ferber, Coach Ferrick, Coach Gibson, Mr. Allen Haines, Coach Matthews, Coach Sader, Coach Straub, Coach Triantos, Coach Wilson, Coach Jon Wingfield, Pastor Gifford, and the University of Maryland coaching staff- Thank you for so much time and effort invested in me and for impacting my life.

Oh yeah… and Chris Rose.

About the Author

Ryan Shieh is a baseball player, Areacode athlete, Liberty University commit, and senior from Upper Marlboro, Maryland who attends Bishop McNamara High School. Ryan's true passion is helping others and promoting Christ in society. He hopes to one day start a foundation that focuses on serving children in need around the world through faith, hope, and love.

Want to contact Ryan? You can reach his email at ryanshieh36@gmail.com. For questions about faith, more on the book, or even if you want to be involved in a Bible verse group chat, please reach out to him!

Follow Ryan on Instagram and Twitter: @ryshieh_